D0558388

Tend My Flock

Kate Litchfield is Diocesan Counsellor for the Diocese of Norwich in the Church of England.

Related titles available from the Canterbury Press

Being a Priest Today: Exploring Priestly Identity
Rosalind Brown and Christopher Cocksworth
'an inspiration to ordinands and a help to priests in finding renewed
focus and confidence in their calling'   *Theology*

Being a Deacon Today
Rosalind Brown

*Diverse Gifts: Varieties of Lay and Ordained Ministries in the Church
and Community*
ed. Malcolm Torry
'This book will be especially helpful to anyone involved
in a local church and who is thinking of ministry in any form'
Professor David Ford

*A Pastoral Prayer Book: For Times of Change, Concern and
Celebration*
Raymond Chapman
'All engaged in pastoralia, but especially priests, will value this most
helpful collection of short liturgies, readings and prayers'   *Search*

www.scm-canterburypress.co.uk

Tend My Flock

Sustaining good pastoral care

Kate Litchfield

CANTERBURY
PRESS
Norwich

© Kate Litchfield 2006

First published in 2006 by the Canterbury Press Norwich
(a publishing imprint of Hymns Ancient & Modern Limited,
a registered charity)
9–17 St Alban's Place, London N1 0NX

www.scm-canterburypress.co.uk

All rights reserved. No part of this publication may be
reproduced, stored in a retrieval system, or transmitted,
in any form or by any means, electronic, mechanical,
photocopying or otherwise, without the prior permission of
the publisher, Canterbury Press.

The Author has asserted her right under the Copyright,
Designs and Patents Act, 1988, to be identified as the
Author of this Work

Scripture quotations are from the New Revised Standard
Version of the Bible, copyright 1989 by the Division of
Christian Education of the National Council of the Churches
of Christ in the USA. Used by permission. All rights reserved.

British Library Cataloguing in Publication data

A catalogue record for this book is available
from the British Library

ISBN 1-85311-648-3/978-1-85311-648-3

Typeset by Regent Typesetting, London
Printed and bound in Great Britain by
William Clowes Ltd, Beccles, Suffolk

Contents

To Jennifer and Malcolm Menin,
in thankfulness for faith and friendship.

All royalties from this book will benefit the work of the Diocese of Norwich.

Foreword

As I look back on my theological training more than thirty years ago, much less attention was given to pastoral studies than to biblical theology, doctrine and church history. It was as if pastoring came naturally and was something you picked up as you began to do your ordained work. There's a sense in which this is true. Nothing teaches like experience. There's a wealth of pastoral care offered by ordained ministers and lay people alike. It's one of the strengths of the Church. But much damage has been done to the Church and the Christian gospel by bad or neglectful pastoring of God's people. That's why this book is of such significance. It is the product of many years spent listening to and reflecting upon the experience in pastoral ministry of both ordained and lay ministers. It will be of immense value for those starting out in their pastoral work. It will be of equal value for those who are experienced already, experienced enough to know how much they still have to learn.

This book does not contain a list of rules to be remembered. It explores the culture, character and circumstances of pastoral ministry for ordained and lay ministers in the Church today. It also explores the care and support which ministers themselves need, if they are to sustain pastoral ministry over many years. I am very grateful to Kate Litchfield, not only for her ministry in this diocese, but for all she has done, with the support of Bishop David Atkinson and others, in the production of this work. I hope that it will find its way into the hands of many who are engaged in pastoral ministry. I am sure it will be of benefit to the Church and its proclamation of the gospel in the coming years.

Graham Norvic
The Right Reverend Graham James
Bishop of Norwich

Acknowledgements

The original version of *Tend My Flock*, published in 1996, was a small booklet for the Diocese of Norwich. It was the vision and inspiration of Canon Paul Oliver who, recognizing a need for practical pastoral guidance for clergy, led the project through a careful process of consultation within the diocese. *Tend My Flock* immediately received national attention and there was a steady demand for copies from dioceses and theological training courses. Other dioceses have, with permission, produced their own versions with variations to suit local need.

I am extremely grateful for the generous support of Paul Oliver who, on behalf of the working party which produced the original *Tend My Flock*, gave permission for me to develop and expand the text, while retaining the title. Paul, encouraged by the then Bishop of Norwich, Peter Nott, led the working party with a wisdom and insight grounded in a lifetime of costly and reflective pastoral ministry. His example has continued to be an inspiration as I have worked on the revised text. Although *Tend My Flock* has been completely rewritten, it incorporates material from the first publication and is recognizably its offspring. While I take full responsibility for the limitations of this new version, I hope that it remains true to the intention and ethos of that pioneering publication.

I am very grateful to our present Bishop of Norwich, Graham James, for encouraging national publication and for writing the Foreword. I am also deeply indebted to the Bishop of Thetford, David Atkinson, for his patient encouragement, clarity of thought and sensitivity to the spirit of the revision. Without his wisdom and steady guidance this book would never have reached completion. The Revd Dr Richard Hines and Canon Vivien Elphick

offered helpful and constructive criticism in the early stages and
Bishop David and Vivien have made written contributions which
I have incorporated into the text. Many other colleagues and
friends have offered valuable suggestions and provided helpful
comments on the draft manuscript.

The Diocese of Norwich, in which I work, is typical of many
rural dioceses. It has many multi-parish rural benefices where
small congregations struggle to survive, while the majority of the
population live in urban and suburban parishes. There are some
urban priority areas, but we lack the ethnic and cultural diversity
of larger cities and conurbations and although many of the
issues raised in this book are applicable across a wide variety of
parishes, I have not attempted to address specific issues outside
my experience.

I write as a lay woman in full-time ministry in the Church of
England. I also write from the perspective of a professional background in counselling and social work. As a counsellor, working
with clergy and members of their families and employed by the
diocese, I share some of the potential hazards of dual relationships (that is, interacting with another person in more than one
role). However, I am also aware of the boundaries which protect
me from many of the complexities which ministers, particularly
those in ordained ministry, have to negotiate on a daily basis.
Counselling, as it has developed from the late twentieth century,
has an important contribution to make in enabling individuals to
find healing from the wounds which damaging childhood experiences or later life events can inflict. However, professional help
can never be a substitute for the healing and supportive relationships provided by family, friends and colleagues, nor for the
pastoral care which should be an inherent part of the life of a
Christian community. Where professional expertise, such as
counselling, becomes necessary, it will be far more effective when
the person being counselled (whether lay or ordained) is held
safely within the network of loving relationships and sustaining
pastoral care which the faith community can and should offer.

In my role as a diocesan counsellor I have been sustained and
stimulated by the friendship of my colleague Dr Roger Hennessey
and by colleagues and friends, who have given encouragement
and support over many years and helped to ensure that our work

continued. For twenty years I have spent much of my time listening to and supporting clergy and members of their families as they have shared with me the costs and joys of ministry. This has been an enriching experience and a great privilege. I have unbounded respect for their commitment to serve God and to care for others with integrity. This book draws upon their experiences and could not have been written without their courage and honesty in sharing with me the pain and rewards of this calling. I hope their trust will be repaid and that it will be a source of practical support to those who share in pastoral ministry.

Over the years, as I have tried to make sense of complex situations and experiences, I have absorbed and reflected upon ideas from many sources, which have become woven into my thinking. I am grateful for these insights, but take responsibility for any errors of interpretation. I have endeavoured to give due acknowledgement to my sources in the text, but would wish to be informed of any omissions so that these can be made good in any future edition.

Kate Litchfield
Diocese of Norwich
Ash Wednesday 2006

Introduction

Jesus said to Simon Peter, 'Simon son of John, do you love me more than these?' He said to him, 'Yes, Lord; you know that I love you.' Jesus said to him, 'Feed my lambs.' A second time he said to him, 'Simon son of John, do you love me?' He said to him, 'Yes, Lord; you know that I love you.' Jesus said to him, 'Tend my sheep.' He said to him the third time, 'Simon son of John, do you love me?' Peter felt hurt because he said to him the third time, 'Do you love me?' And he said to him, 'Lord, you know everything; you know that I love you.' Jesus said to him, 'Feed my sheep.'

John 21.15–17

Tend My Flock is a companion and guide for ordained and lay ministers who are seeking to be faithful to their calling and to live well, amid all the complexities and pressures of pastoral ministry in contemporary society. It addresses some of the issues in pastoral ministry which too often remain unspoken. It raises questions and suggests approaches which could be helpful in making sense of complex and confusing situations. It also contains much that is relevant to the experience of spouses and other close relatives of ministers, whose lives are often deeply affected by the minister's vocation, but who can feel isolated and alone, particularly if they are unfamiliar with the culture of Anglican ministry. I hope it might also be useful to counsellors and therapists working with clergy and their relatives.

Tend My Flock does not attempt to be a comprehensive guide to pastoral care or to provide the last word on the topics explored. Rather it invites dialogue, reflection, honest self-examination and the courage to share struggles and dilemmas with colleagues, friends in ministry and family members. Above all its aim is to enable ministers and those close to them to live their pastoral ministry well. While it is written from an Anglican perspective, with Anglican terminology, most of the issues addressed are common to pastoral ministers of other denominations.

Throughout the Church there is an immense amount of excellent pastoral care provided by ministers, ordained and lay, who, with integrity and sensitivity, communicate God's love by offering help and support to those who are vulnerable and in need. Much of this pastoral care, which reaches well beyond the faith community, goes unseen and unrecognized.

Ordained pastoral ministry is a particular calling of great privilege and of rich variety and opportunity. It can bring those who minister much fulfilment and joy. Many clergy would not want to be doing anything else. They find it immensely rewarding to be alongside others at crucial times in their journey through life and to share with them the good news of God's love. They also gain great satisfaction from enabling others to share with them the privilege of pastoral ministry. However, pastoral ministry is a vocation with risks and vulnerabilities for, whatever our calling, we are all frail human beings who make mistakes and sometimes fail. It is also a vocation which can be costly for close relatives and friends of ministers.

Tend My Flock is therefore written with an awareness of both the privilege and the risks involved in pastoral ministry. That is why the story of Peter's betrayal of his promise to be faithful to Christ, his repentance, forgiveness and commissioning supply the title. We can see in the life and ministry of Peter that it is not our betrayal of Christ that isolates us from each other and separates us from God, but our inability to face up to our betrayals, to learn from them and to allow costly repentance and loving forgiveness to penetrate heart, mind and spirit. We can also see from Christ's determination to trust Peter again, despite his betrayal, that when we have been let down by others we too may need to take the costly risk of trusting again. This can be hard for ministers, who sometimes get hurt by harshly given criticism and who understandably seek to protect themselves from further hurt. It can also be hard for those to whom they minister, disillusioned at discovering that their ministers are ordinary human beings who fail and get things wrong.

Reading this book may, at times, stir up uncomfortable thoughts and feelings about mistakes and failures in ministry. But it is written with a conviction that it is only when we believe that we are better than we are, deny our weaknesses or isolate ourselves in shame and despair at our betrayals that we place ourselves outside the reach of the healing and redemptive love of God, mediated to us through friends, family, colleagues and those to whom we minister. When we can face ourselves, our mistakes and the damage we have done and seek forgiveness, then redemption is possible for us and for those whom we have hurt. This does not in any way excuse or justify bad or unethical practice, let alone the abuse of those who are vulnerable, but it is recognition that, for anyone engaged in pastoral ministry over any length of time, there will be things we get wrong and things we could have done so much better. One of the paradoxes of ministry is that those ministers who have honestly and in humility faced up to their failures and betrayals, sometimes become the most pastorally sensitive and effective, with a ministry deeply enriched by painful confrontation with their own wounded humanity. We all love imperfectly and we all hurt even those we love most and most want to serve. But it is when we have the courage to face our broken humanity and be vulnerable that God is able to work through us far more powerfully than when we are relying too much on our own human strength. We are much more likely to get into difficulties and betray our calling when, like Peter, we are so confident and enthusiastic that we overreach ourselves or claim to be more competent and resilient than we are.

Tend My Flock is also written with an awareness that those who get things badly wrong, causing untold damage in the way they minister, have almost always set out with high hopes and ideals. Usually the slide into unethical or abusive practice happens gradually, with the small acts of self-deception and compromise that we are all prone to. Naming some of the issues, particularly those which are seldom talked about in ministry, may help to overcome the fear which can isolate ministers and prevent them from acknowledging vulnerability to colleagues or to those they serve. The hope is that the reflections offered in this book, the practical suggestions made and the questions raised, will encourage self-awareness and realism about the risks inherent in pastoral ministry.

The book focuses not only on areas of risk but also on how ministers can sustain their ministry by taking proper care of their own needs for rest, relaxation and support. It also encourages discussion between the minister and those close to them about the impact of ministry on their pattern of life and relationships. In this there is recognition that we are all members of the flock that needs tending. All who are called to offer pastoral care to others also need to receive love and care and to learn an appropriate love and care for themselves and their families, if they are to remain faithful to their calling and to minister in ways that are life enhancing. Loneliness, isolation and the insulation that comes when we protect ourselves from hurt often lie behind poor pastoral practice. Pastoral care cannot be done without support from other people and is never one-way.

Theological reflection, the sacraments, prayer and meditation are also vital. Self-awareness can grow through a willingness to examine our inner responses to people and situations in the light of Scripture and with the help of insights into human emotional and psychological development. This process needs time for prayer and reflection in solitude, but it cannot be done in isolation. True self-understanding is always discovered in community, in the context of our relationships with other people. There are some aspects of ourselves that we simply cannot see for ourselves. We need someone else to hold up the mirror and reflect back to us the parts that they can see but which are hidden from our view. This demands a context of trust in which we can let go of fear and feel safe enough to explore and share our fear and self-doubts with others. The danger for ministers, particularly those who are ordained, is that their position of authority may insulate them from the kind of honest feedback from other people which we all need if we are to grow in self-awareness. When criticism comes in a form that is so disguised that it provides no useful information, the minister is deprived of valuable insights into how their behaviour affects other people. When it is given in ways that are hurtful and bewildering, then he or she may retreat from authentic encounter in order to avoid further pain. We all need to experience loving acceptance if we are to risk revealing our true selves.

Then we may learn to allow others to confront us, in love, with those aspects of ourselves that cause difficulty in our ministerial relationships.

This guide is not only about recognizing areas of difficulty. It can also be used to create opportunities to affirm our own and other ministers' good pastoral practice. There is a place for reflecting carefully and prayerfully on an aspect of ministry, checking out our perceptions with others and acknowledging that it is an area where we function well. Specific positive feedback and thoughtful encouragement play a crucial role in building up confidence and energizing us to meet new challenges. Ministers who receive affirmation and discover how encouraging it is are more likely to give affirmation to those they serve. Parishioners who feel affirmed by their ministers are also more likely to respond to them with encouragement. In church life we often fail to encourage or express our appreciation to one another, but we all need affirmation from others to sustain us in ministry, particularly through the inevitable times of discouragement. Identifying what we and other ministers do well and why something has been successful is a vital part of becoming more effective in ministry.

Notes

- 'Minister' is used to include both lay and ordained ministers.
- 'Ordained minister' is used when focusing on issues specific to clergy.
- 'Parish' and 'benefice' are used interchangeably.
- 'Area dean' and 'rural dean' are used interchangeably.

Ways of Using this Book

Who is this book for?

Tend My Flock is designed to be used by:

- ordained and lay ministers
- anyone considering training for ordination or lay ministry
- theological training courses
- training courses for lay ministry
- training incumbents and curates
- continuing ministerial education programmes
- clergy preparing to take up senior appointments
- family members or close friends of ministers or prospective ministers
- counsellors working with clergy and members of their families.

Personal study and reflection

The guide does not have to be read consecutively, but the introduction should be read first, and then:

- each chapter stands alone but there is a progression through the book
- one or two sections may be sufficient to reflect upon at any one time
- choose those that seem most relevant, don't attempt to work through too many
- questions are for personal reflection and prayer, but not all are suitable for group discussion

- keeping a journal of reflections can be a helpful way of exploring issues more deeply
- the book can be used as a personal record, with the reader adding comments, reflections, Bible or other references to the text
- issues arising from personal reflection and prayer could be explored further with a spiritual guide, counsellor, ministerial consultant or supervisor
- issues arising from personal reflection and prayer could be talked over with family members, friends or peer colleagues in ministry.

Use in groups

Specific topics from *Tend My Flock* could be used with a variety of groups including:

- pastoral care reflection groups on theological training courses
- continuing ministerial education groups for curates
- training courses for training incumbents
- ministry teams
- clergy chapter meetings
- clergy peer support groups
- senior staff groups
- churchwardens
- diocesan support staff
- marriage partners or others with whom the minister shares their life
- groups set up specifically to study *Tend My Flock*
- support or supervision groups for counsellors working with clergy and their relatives.

Guidelines for group use

Participants and group leaders should all read through the Introduction and these guidelines before making a commitment to use the book together.

Choosing a topic for discussion

Although each chapter stands alone and chapters can be read and studied in any order, each chapter topic also builds on what has gone before. It is important to recognize that issues discussed in this guide, for example confidentiality, power or gender, are not abstract topics, but will be present in the dynamics of the group. Topics which are potentially more threatening, for example over-involvement with parishioners or colleagues, sexual abuse issues or loss and bereavement, need to be dealt with after a sufficient level of trust has been established in the group and with the agreement of all participants. Not all sections are suitable for group discussion; some are more appropriate for individual reflection or one-to-one discussion, and leaders and participants need to use discernment about this. Certain topics may also be unsuitable for a particular group, especially a group that is not self-selected, where people could feel under more pressure. It will therefore be safer if participants can choose topics rather than having them imposed or working through the book section by section. If a participant wishes to opt out of discussion on a particular subject this should always be respected.

'Health' warning

Some issues may stir up difficult feelings in the participants. Although participants should read through a topic and reflect upon the questions beforehand, the questions are primarily intended for private reflection and some would be inappropriate for use in a group setting.

Creating a safe environment

Mutual encouragement and deeper sharing depend on whether participants feel safe enough to be open and honest with one another. Learning for everyone will depend on full participation, but this should never be forced. Discussion in the group should be allowed to flow naturally, with participants sharing in their own time. There will be more potential for learning together if participants feel safe enough to acknowledge mistakes, difficulties or areas of uncertainty in their ministry, but establishing this level of trust takes time and commitment from all the group members. Safety can be undermined by irregular attendance, poor time boundaries and lack of clarity about confidentiality.

The following suggestions for safe boundaries of confidentiality should be discussed and established from the beginning and reviewed when a new member joins the group:

- anything shared by others within the group should be confidential
- no discussion outside the group of other participants' style of participating
- anything shared in subgroups or pairs should be confidential, unless a participant chooses to share their own material in the full group
- anyone unable to attend should not expect others to report on what has been said within the group in their absence
- no discussion in the group about anyone who is not present at a particular meeting.

Clear time boundaries also provide safety:

- begin and end on time
- allow sufficient time for in-depth discussion without the danger of overrunning
- consider having a pilot session
- after the pilot session make a commitment to meet on a specific number of occasions
- review whether participants wish to continue at the end of the agreed number of sessions.

If a group has a pre-existing membership (e.g. a ministry team or deanery chapter), or is set up as part of a training course, then it is particularly important that everyone feels they have a choice about how they participate. Effective learning depends on finding a balance between taking risks and respecting limits. Participants should always be allowed to take responsibility for how much they share. No one should be put under pressure to speak about a specific issue. If the material is used on training courses then particular attention should be given to how issues of assessment could undermine safety within the group.

Size of group

Groups will vary in size, depending on whether there is a pre-existing membership or the group is convened specifically for the purpose of studying *Tend My Flock*.

- study and discussion could involve as few as three or four colleagues, in which case leadership and facilitation would be shared informally between them
- a group of up to eight participants could function with one leader or facilitator
- a group of twelve is the maximum for effective discussion and would benefit from two leaders or facilitators
- in a larger group it may sometimes help to break up into twos or threes.

Leaders or facilitators

Leaders or facilitators may be from outside the group membership. If leadership is from within the group then it may be best if it is shared among group members. Participants could volunteer to lead discussion on a particular topic that interests or is of concern to them. The leader or facilitator should:

- ensure that the meeting starts and finishes on time and it may also be their responsibility to lead prayer and choose the Bible reading
- keep the focus on the topic under discussion and discourage flight into abstract theories or theological disputes
- ensure there is sensitive follow-up for anyone who appears to be disturbed or distressed during or as a result of the discussion
- ensure that no participant's personal experience is denied, even if it is not shared
- ensure that nobody is pressurized into contributing if they choose not to speak
- ensure that everyone has a chance to speak if they wish to and that no one monopolizes the discussion.

Participants

All participants should:

- read and reflect upon the Introduction
- undertake to read and reflect upon the sections to be discussed
- make a commitment to arrive on time, not to leave early and to give priority to regular attendance at the group, even if they sometimes find the sessions difficult or there are other competing demands on their time
- safeguard confidentiality when talking about a specific situation they have encountered; names and identifying details should be excluded
- endeavour to speak out of their personal experience rather than taking refuge in abstract theories or displays of theological expertise
- take particular responsibility for safeguarding themselves, if a topic feels potentially unsafe or threatening
- offer active listening; it may sometimes be more appropriate to receive a contribution with silence or a simple acknowledgement, rather than comment, question or counter-argument
- be ready to affirm other people's individual experience and perceptions, even if they are not shared
- respect different theological perspectives and points of view.

A framework of Bible reading and prayer

An appropriate and short Bible reading and prayer at the beginning and/or end of the session can help to create a safe and containing framework and ensure that discussion is rooted in shared faith. If there is vocal prayer at the end, care should be taken not to use it as a way of continuing or responding to the earlier discussion. For this reason silence and a brief closing prayer may be the safest way of bringing the session to a close.

I

Aspects of Pastoral Care

The gifts he gave were that some would be apostles, some prophets, some evangelists, some pastors and teachers, to equip the saints for the work of ministry, for building up the body of Christ, until all of us come to the unity of the faith and of the knowledge of the Son of God, to maturity, to the measure of the full stature of Christ.

Ephesians 4.11–13

1.1 Defining pastoral care

Through baptism all God's people have a gift of ministry from the ascended Christ to be offered for the good of the whole Body of Christ. The heart of all ministry is self-giving love and the priestly ministry of all Christians is to enable one another to be brought into touch with the loving heart of God (Eph. 4).

Pastoral care is central to the life of the Church and determined by the command to love God with heart and soul and mind and one's neighbour as oneself. This implies a reciprocal response, as people are enabled both to receive and to give love (Campbell 1985). Christians believe that love lies at the heart of God and that Jesus Christ is the incarnation of that love. So Christians, committed to the belief that God loves us all unconditionally, seek to reflect the love of God for each unique human being (Wright 1982).

The fundamental aim of pastoral care is the enactment of this love, incorporating the pastoral functions of healing, sustaining, guiding and reconciling witnessed in the priestly ministry of Jesus and in the life of the early Church (Clebsch and Jeakle 1994).

These aspects of pastoral care may be expressed in a wide

variety of activities, involving individuals, groups and communities and undertaken from within the faith community. It is not only about responding to problems but also encompasses the celebration of what is good:

> . . . it is also about sharing in community, feasting in friendship, exchanging mutual support . . . Pastoral care may include befriending, promoting self-help activities, giving material aid, creating opportunities for increased learning, campaigning, protesting against unjust events and structures, pastoral education, community development, crisis management and conflict mediation. (Diocesan Advisers in Pastoral Care and Counselling 1995)

Liturgy is also an expression of pastoral care, enabling worshippers to connect their individual stories with the story of God's love for his people; every aspect of public worship will contribute to an image of God as one who invites, includes and empowers or who appears to do the reverse. Liturgy shapes the church community and should enable the whole people of God to fulfil a richly varied ministry of pastoral care regardless of education or social background (Green 1987). Administration is also an important aspect of pastoral ministry, communicating respect and care when it is done well.

The spectrum of pastoral care may range from simple acts of spontaneous kindness to planned interventions, which, while firmly rooted in theological understanding, may also draw on the insights of secular disciplines, such as social work, counselling and community development (Campbell 1985). Although pastoral care is therefore both a corporate and an individual activity, this book will focus primarily on ministry to individuals on their own, or within their family, friendship or community network.

1.2 Differentiating pastoral care and counselling

Since the latter half of the twentieth century counselling and psychotherapy as specific disciplines, contained within the wider range of pastoral care activities, have had a profound influence on the care that ministers (particularly those who are ordained) offer to individuals. This influence brings both valuable insights and potential hazards.

The original meaning of the word 'counselling' is rooted in the Christian tradition of pastoral care. Its appropriation to describe a specific therapeutic activity is a late-twentieth-century development which has become widely accepted as counselling has become professionalized. Unfortunately, as pastoral ministry has been increasingly influenced by the developing role of the secular professional counsellor, there has been a tendency to lose the distinction between pastoral care and counselling and to undervalue pastoral care as an activity in its own right (Bridger and Atkinson 1994). It is essential to be aware that, while all ordained ministers are pastoral carers, not all are counsellors in the contemporary secular sense. It is also important to recognize that, although counsellors can enable their clients' exploration of spiritual issues, this does not make them pastors. They too need to be aware of their limitations and to recognize the skills, knowledge and experience of the ordained minister.

Christopher Moody, in his book *Eccentric Ministry* (1992), distinguishes between pastoral care and counselling, exploring how the ordained minister's role is to create a living contact between the tradition of the faith community and the individual's experience. Sometimes the minister will do very little, other than to be a presence at times of crisis or loss of meaning in people's lives, perhaps being a recipient of their anger with God, or enabling those who do not believe to catch a glimpse of the gracious activity of God. While counselling and therapy tend to be individualistic in approach, the ordained minister will see pastoral ministry in the wider context of a relationship with God and with the faith community, and may offer pastoral advice, spiritual counsel, prayer and sacramental ministry. Unlike secular professional counselling, which has clearly defined boundaries of time and place, pastoral care of individuals may occur in many formal and informal settings. The informality of pastoral care is one of its assets in a society where most professional help is formalized and given by appointment. In contrast, pastoral care can seem untidy and ill-defined, but it is probably much closer to the messy reality of people's lives, where they share their troubles when they can and often do so under the cover of a noisy television, on a car journey, at the pub or when meeting by chance on their way somewhere else. Such spontaneity requires availability and will not happen if the minister's diary is always packed with formal appointments.

Pastoral care may be in one-to-one encounter or involve other church and family members and friends. Unlike a counselling relationship, a pastoral care relationship may be initiated by the minister and the minister will be known as a person with other relationships within the faith community. Meetings may be in a person's home, rather than church premises, and friendship may become a dimension of this caring ministry.

However, confusion can arise because, with an ever-increasing demand for personal counselling and the lack of affordable counselling services, people may turn to their ordained minister for a form of help which may go well beyond the normal expectations of pastoral care. If the minister engages with areas of experience beyond their competence, the consequences may be damaging for all concerned. Confusion can also occur when terms such as 'Christian counselling' and 'prayer counselling' are used in the Church. Ministers need to be clear about the difference between these activities and counselling as understood in a secular context. Ministers who are not trained as counsellors should be careful not to confuse their pastoral ministry with that of counselling or psychotherapy.

1.3 Listening and counselling skills

Listening well is fundamental to all good pastoral care. Insights from and training in counselling skills can improve communication and make a valuable contribution to pastoral care. Such training can enhance ministers' ability to listen at depth and increase their self-awareness and capacity to discern accurately. The insights of the person-centred approach to counselling, emphasizing the value of empathy, warmth, acceptance and genuineness in all helping relationships, can enhance a minister's ability to offer parishioners an environment in which they can feel heard and understood (Rogers 1979).

1.4 Clergy with counselling training

Those ordained ministers who have a professional training as counsellor or therapist need to reflect carefully upon issues of ethics and good practice before deciding whether or not to add this dimension, with appropriate boundaries and explanation, to the pastoral care they offer in the parish. While ministers who have counselling training to an accredited standard will draw on this in the pastoral care they offer parishioners, they need always to consider carefully what kind of support is being sought or offered and what is appropriate. They should also clarify this with the parishioner seeking help. Otherwise confusion may arise in the minds of both minister and parishioner as to which role the minister is in. The minister should always be clear whether he or she is working with a parishioner as a counsellor and only do so if there has been explicit agreement to this. Both need to be aware of how authority deriving from the ordained minister's role may affect the counselling relationship (2.3; 2.9). They also need to discuss the implications of establishing a dual relationship (relating to each other in more than one role) and of how a counselling relationship between them might affect their contact in other contexts (3.5). The minister (whether ordained or lay) who is also a trained counsellor should consider carefully whether counselling as currently understood should be carried out within the parish context, or whether it would be more appropriate within a voluntary counselling agency. If a minister also works as counsellor, there are important questions to consider regarding accreditation, supervision and specific ethical requirements (see pp. 32–4).

1.5 Ordained ministry, vocation and profession

The particular calling from God to the ordained priesthood of the Church is expressed in service, intercession and self-giving love. It is a ministry of Word, sacrament and pastoral care, a divine gift enabling the whole Church to exercise its priestly ministry. The vocation to ordained ministry is a free response to the call to commit oneself to love and serve God and so to love and serve others (Gula 1996). This means that 'the sense that they are engaged in a vocation rather than a career is fundamental to the clergy's identity and self-understanding' (Bridger 2003).

Originally, within the context of the religious life, having a vocation and making a profession were inseparable. Even without such religious associations, the link between vocation and profession continued in the ideal of dedicated commitment to serve others, expected in vocational professions such as medicine, nursing or teaching. However, for some the term 'professional' now carries negative connotations, implying attitudes of detachment, or of seeking status and financial reward. As a result some clergy may be reluctant to identify their calling with being 'professional'. Nevertheless, in contemporary society, acting in a professional way continues to bring the expectation of commitment to the acquisition of expert knowledge and skill to be used in dedicated service to others. Identifying 'vocation' with being 'professional' should therefore be seen as an affirmation of the need for high standards of competence and integrity in ministry and a motivation to work out what this means in practice in all the complexities of our contemporary society (Gula 1996). Increasingly the Church of England is adopting an approach that affirms this expectation of 'professionalism', but in attempting to legislate for this, there is the risk that the creative flexibility of ministry could be undermined.

The increasing number of non-stipendiary and ordained local ministers working in a voluntary capacity also raises important questions about the values, duties and responsibilities inherent in regarding ministry as a profession as well as a vocation, even though it may be undertaken on a voluntary basis.

1.6 Covenant relationships

Richard M. Gula (1996), writing in *Ethics in Pastoral Ministry*, explores the important differences between contract and covenant relationships.

Secular models of professional relationship are increasingly defined by explicit contract, specifying the rights and duties of the parties involved and the service offered. In contrast, what is asked of ministers cannot be worked out in advance and defined by contract. Pastoral care requires flexibility, spontaneity and a readiness to respond to the unexpected. It is rooted in the biblical model of covenant, exemplified by the covenant relationship between God and God's people. This is a relationship of gracious love in which God, who loves us freely and infinitely, calls us to be generous in our loving service to others. Covenant relationships in pastoral care always take place in the context of the minister's relationship with God and the Christian community, even though the person receiving pastoral care may not be a member of that community or share faith in God.

The covenant nature of pastoral relationships means that the minister does not prescribe in advance what will be offered. The minister allows his or her ministry to be a response to the specific need of the other person, who entrusts their vulnerability to the minister. The risk for both is that the minister will be tempted to offer a service beyond his or her abilities, or one that is inappropriate or even damaging. A covenant relationship therefore places a heavy responsibility on the minister to develop moral discernment and sensitivity in distinguishing between loving and unloving behaviour in ministerial relationships, and to be self-aware about his or her own limitations. This requires a discipline of prayer and reflection and a willingness to be self-questioning and transparent about motives, needs and vulnerabilities. It is too easy for a minister to delude him- or herself that actions are motivated by love, and to be unaware of deeper and more questionable motives underlying seemingly benevolent acts. Pastoral care must always be directed towards the well-being of the person who seeks help. Even within the flexibility of the covenant relationship the minister's practice must still be to a professional standard.

1.7 Ordained and lay ministers as exemplars

Ministers, as the public face of both the local congregation and the wider Church, must accept a responsibility to maintain public confidence in the role of the minister and trust in the integrity of the Church. The parish priest and other ministers in public office are never free from the moral and spiritual requirements of office, even when not on duty. All ministers, lay or ordained, are called to be servants on behalf of Jesus Christ, the Servant of all, and their authority is rooted in Christ. The Church therefore rightly expects certain standards of behaviour from its public representatives, who are seen as role models for the Christian life of faith.

Society is rightly critical of people who claim certain standards and then fail to live up to them. Individual failures are also likely to be exploited by some sections of the media, diminishing the credibility and authority of the Church. However, ministers share the frailties common to all human beings. They put themselves and others at great risk if they lose touch with this reality and start to believe that they are somehow different and less susceptible to mistakes and failures. Ministers have to learn how to live in the tension between realism about their vulnerable humanity and acceptance of the often difficult burden of being seen as an example.

At the heart of all effective ministry is the nurturing of discipleship in openness to God, through prayer, Scripture, sacrament and a readiness to discern the movement of the Holy Spirit. No human being can adequately fulfil the model of ministry seen in Jesus. But he is our priest and,

> we do not have a high priest who is unable to sympathise with our weaknesses, but we have one who in every respect has been tested as we are, yet without sin. Let us therefore approach the throne of grace with boldness, so that we may receive mercy and find grace to help in time of need. (Heb. 4.15–16)

1.8 Accountability in ministry

The concept of accountability is common to management and to Christian ministry, although it may be interpreted differently. A minister is a servant of Christ, who is the head of his body the Church, and a minister's ultimate accountability is to God. However, at a human level, accountability in ministry is complex, encompassing the person being ministered to and those close to them, colleagues in ministry, the bishop and the wider Church. A sense of accountability to oneself and to one's family is also crucial. Specifically, ordained ministers are accountable to the Church, through the bishop, whose ministry is properly understood as a shared ministry, and expressed in the licensing or institution charge as 'both yours and mine'.

1.9 Sacred trust

Ministry is entrusted to us by God. Ministers are called to be trustworthy.

They are often in situations where people are at physical, emotional or spiritual risk and therefore extremely vulnerable. People turn to them when they are at their most vulnerable, at times of joy and celebration, or of profound distress, in the aftermath of traumatic experiences, when facing personal dilemmas or struggling with guilt and remorse. The ordained minister may also have privileged access to places (e.g. prisons and hospitals) and be invited to be present in circumstances where access is normally restricted. It is only through the vital element of trust, the sign of Christ's compassion entrusted to his Church, that these opportunities for pastoral care to those in great distress are made possible. If this trust is damaged it can affect the wider Church over generations.

Reflection – the pastoral role

- What do you value most about your pastoral role? What opportunities and challenges does it offer that would not be possible for a counsellor?
- How flexible are you in responding to unexpected pastoral opportunities?
- What are your experiences of being listened to accurately and at depth? How well do you listen?
- Do you see ordained ministry as a 'profession' and how does this influence your ministry, whether paid or voluntary, ordained or lay?

- What are the tensions between ordained ministry as vocation and contemporary expectations about career development?
- What are the risks and challenges for you of understanding pastoral care as a covenant relationship?
- In which areas of your life do you find it hard to live up to the expectations that you or others have of you as a Christian minister?

1.10 Confidentiality and trust

Confidentiality is crucial to the development of trust in pastoral care. This applies not only to situations where the expectation of confidentiality is clear, but also to the many informal pastoral contacts that ministers have, where they may be given information because of their role and because they are trusted. In a pastoral relationship self-disclosure to the minister makes the person vulnerable, and increases the minister's power in relation to him or her. Ministers need to be sensitive to the way they hold this power. If the minister keeps firm boundaries around confidentiality this enables the vulnerable person to retain control over their life. Breaches of, or leaks in, confidentiality disempower a person by undermining their ability to control what other people know about them (Gula 1996). Where dual roles and relationships are involved there needs to be particular sensitivity to confidentiality (3.5). For example, if an ordinand is also an employee of the diocese they may feel very vulnerable about information being passed, without their knowledge, between tutors on their training course and diocesan staff. In such circumstances transparency is essential and the complex boundaries of confidentiality should be discussed and mutually agreed from the start.

1.11 Context and confidentiality

Ministers should reflect upon how information received in one setting affects their relationship with a person in other situations. They also need to be very aware of how easy it is, even if unintentionally, to misuse confidential information. This can happen in private conversation with colleagues, lay ministry team members, or friends within the parish community, or even with the person concerned, in a different context.

Explicit clarification on confidentiality and reassurance that on meeting in a different context nothing will be raised, alluded to or, as it were, 'known' or 'remembered' by the minister, helps people feel safer. Amid many other preoccupations the minister who has received many personal disclosures may find it easy to set aside or forget what has been divulged. It is therefore important for all ministers to remain sensitive to the reality that, for the person who has disclosed personal information, perhaps for the first or only time in their life, the memory of that disclosure will always remain vivid. In consequence, feelings of vulnerability are likely to persist for a very long time after the disclosure was made. The person may therefore be particularly sensitive to any perceived criticism, avoidance or withdrawal on the part of the minister. They may easily and understandably misinterpret behaviour which is, in reality, the result of the minister's other preoccupations or tiredness.

1.12 Clergy and confidentiality

Information shared in confidence with an ordained person must, in all but the most exceptional circumstances (1.13; 1.16; pp. 34–5), be regarded as confidential and only divulged with the other person's properly informed consent. Learning when and how to hold confidentiality and when and how to share information is an essential part of ministerial formation. However, confidentiality is particularly complex in pastoral care, because information may be obtained in situations and encounters, such as committee meetings or phone conversations, where it may not be so obvious that there is an expectation of confidentiality.

Training incumbents and curates face particular issues of confidentiality which they need to reflect upon together. Some hold the view that assistant clergy in training posts should normally share with their training incumbent information given to them within a parish pastoral context (*Guidelines for the Professional Conduct of Clergy* 2003). If this is the agreed policy then parishioners should be made aware of it. Others would say that the curate should always obtain explicit consent before sharing information with their incumbent and respect any refusal.

Being told other people's secrets can place heavy burdens on the ordained person. Such secrets may involve distressing or disturbing information or may be about experiences of deep spiritual meaning, such as experiences of God, which the person has never dared to share before. All clergy need to learn how to manage the spiritual, emotional and psychological demands which this responsibility to hold confidential information will make on them during the course of their ministry. Clergy who have a ministerial consultant or supervisor, with whom they can share some aspects of their pastoral ministry, may be at less risk of inappropriate and potentially damaging 'leaks' of confidential information which they are finding it difficult to hold safely. However, ministers who have such support still need to adopt safeguards to protect confidentiality. These may include:

- informing the person they are pastoring that they have a ministerial supervisor or consultant with whom they sometimes share information about their ministry
- seeking the person's permission to share in this way, if they might perceive it to be jeopardizing confidentiality
- choosing a supervisor or consultant who has sufficient distance from the minister's pastoral work not to be able to identify whom they are talking about
- disguising names and other details that might reveal the person's identity.

Ministers also need to bear in mind that the Church at both local and national level is a comparatively small community, where relationship networks can easily jeopardize confidentiality, and individuals and their circumstances may be identifiable, even when names are not used. Information divulged under the 'seal of the confessional' cannot be shared with a ministerial supervisor, although it may be possible to discuss underlying issues and principles, but without any reference to the person concerned.

Unless explicit permission has been given, clergy and others involved in pastoral ministry should not share confidential information with their spouses, family or friends. They should also treat information shared among colleagues as confidential (*Guidelines for the Professional Conduct of Clergy* 2003).

1.13 Confession

Canon law imposes an obligation upon the priest not to break 'the seal of the confessional'. A priest who discloses matters revealed in the course of formal confession commits an ecclesiastical offence (except possibly in matters of treason) under the unrepealed Canon 113 of 1603 (Leeder 1999).

> There can be no disclosure of what is confessed to a priest. This principle holds even after the death of the penitent. The priest may not refer to what has been learnt in confession, even to the penitent, unless explicitly permitted. Some appropriate act of contrition and reparation may be necessary before absolution is given. (*Guidelines for the Professional Conduct of the Clergy* 2003)

If a crime or offence is revealed in the particular context of formal confession, the seal of the confessional applies. However, the priest should urge the person to report his or her behaviour to the police or social services and may decide to withhold absolution until they have demonstrated this evidence of repentance (House of Bishops 2004).

It is unclear how far secular courts would consider communication within confession privileged from the requirement to give evidence in court. The weight of current opinion seems to be that confessions made to a minister of religion are not privileged from such disclosure although, in practice, it would seem that the courts respect the tradition of absolute confidentiality (Hill 2001).

If a priest were summoned to give evidence in court and the court held that, despite Canon 113, the priest was not entitled to refuse to answer questions, the Legal Advisory Commission Opinion is that an ecclesiastical offence would not be committed, if the priest then revealed information. However, any priest summoned to give evidence on information received under Canon 113 should seek legal advice. Under the Act of Terrorism 2000 it is unlikely that Canon 113 would be accepted as a defence against the legal requirement to disclose information concerning terrorism (Legal Advisory Commission, forthcoming 2007).

Canon law does not apply to informal pastoral conversations. Therefore confessions should normally be heard at advertised times or in a context which makes a clear distinction between formal confession and 'a general pastoral conversation or a meeting for spiritual direction' (House of Bishops 2004).

Clergy should be aware that there are authorized forms for confession and absolution, in addition to those found in the Book of Common Prayer Visitation of the Sick Service, and that hearing confessions should not be undertaken without specific training and preparation. The authorized Christian Initiation Services also include provision for individual and private penitence, which would constitute formal confession as covered by canon law.

Clarity about confidentiality is essential in those traditions of the Church where formal confession and absolution are not used. For example, the person who shares their story with an ordained person in informal conversation may mistakenly expect the absolute confidentiality offered within the ministry of confession and absolution. However, in this situation confidentiality does not have the protection of canon law.

1.14 Lay ministers and confidentiality

The development of collaborative ministry and ministry teams has brought increasing opportunities for lay ministers to become aware of confidential information. Those sharing pastoral ministry with the incumbent need to have a clear understanding of the requirements of confidentiality. They should not offer absolute confidentiality and need to be aware of and explicit about their responsibility to seek advice, guidance and support. They should seek guidance when faced with ethical dilemmas regarding confidentiality, individuals at risk and the law. If there are allegations of abuse of children or vulnerable adults they should always seek advice from those in the parish or diocese who are responsible for child and adult protection.

1.15 Confidentiality in shared ministry

Where ministry is shared, best practice may be difficult to define. Some professionals, particularly those who are part of a team, take confidentiality to include the right to share with professional colleagues, who may also be working with the person. Members of ministry teams need to discuss their understanding of confidentiality with one another and to make known their policy and practice. While it is important to safeguard the right of parishioners to share personal information with one minister and not another, in a team situation it may be advisable to create an explicit policy of corporate confidentiality. This will protect against the possibility of members of a ministry team being manipulated or divided by the sharing of personal information with one and not another (*Guidelines for the Professional Conduct of Clergy* 2003). Such a policy must, of course, exclude information divulged to an ordained minister in sacramental confession.

Although views and practice may vary, increasingly the expectation is that boundaries of confidentiality should be made explicit and that information will be shared only on a need-to-know basis. The risk of not being explicit about any limits on confidentiality is that the minister may subsequently share information with someone whom the other person regards as inappropriate. This may then be experienced as an extremely damaging breach of trust.

1.16 Confidentiality and conflict of interest

There is not, at present, any mandatory responsibility to disclose information about suspected child abuse to statutory agencies, but there is increasing recognition of a moral responsibility to do so where a child may be at risk of serious harm. Clergy and others, including churchwardens, who hold public office may feel a particular burden of responsibility and find themselves facing complex issues and potential conflicts of interest. This section draws substantially on *Protecting All God's Children* (House of Bishops 2004), which provides a great deal of helpful guidance on issues of confidentiality and is an important resource for ministers.

The Human Rights Act 1998 protects the right to respect for private and family life, home and correspondence. A public authority (which could be an ordained minister) has to have lawful and necessary justification for interfering with this right. The potential harm from not reporting allegations of abuse is likely to be relevant to decisions about what is justified interference. Entitlement to confidentiality is also recognized in law, where information is accepted in confidence, or the nature of the relationship (as between doctor and patient or priest and parishioner) creates a presumption of confidentiality. The law also recognizes that, on rare occasions, other considerations may lead to a professionally responsible decision to breach confidentiality. If there is a risk of harm, either to the person concerned or to others, particularly to vulnerable adults or to children, ministers may consider it their duty to break a confidence. In such instances they will have to decide carefully how to proceed and what the risks are, and should seek advice from the appropriate diocesan adviser. They should not attempt to investigate the situation themselves, nor speak directly to any person against whom allegations have been made.

Children or adults who disclose significant harm need to know that such information will have to be passed to the statutory agency, usually social services, so that it can be properly investigated and further abuse prevented. This will also be necessary where significant harm is suspected. It may not be necessary when an adult discloses historical abuse, unless the alleged abuser is still working with or caring for children, in which case the authorities must be informed. If there is a conflict of interest between a child's need for protection and the needs of an adult, the welfare of the child is paramount.

However, in all but the most exceptional circumstances, good practice requires informing and, wherever possible, obtaining permission, before divulging confidential information to the statutory authorities. If at all possible the person concerned should be encouraged and enabled to make the disclosure themselves.

On rare occasions it may be necessary to inform a person of the disclosure retrospectively. In matters of child protection, or other criminal activity, there may be a risk that, if an alleged perpetrator is pre-warned, they will have the opportunity to destroy evidence or threaten the child or other persons who are at risk. In some very exceptional circumstances it may therefore be necessary to go ahead with disclosure, neither obtaining permission nor informing the person that disclosure has taken place. Ministers should be aware that there is a legal requirement to disclose information where acts of terrorism are concerned (1.13).

All ministers will benefit from careful consideration of the ethical issues involved before such acutely difficult pastoral situations arise. Ministers also need to be aware of and observe national and diocesan guidelines and requirements regarding protection of children and vulnerable adults, and should know how to contact the appropriate diocesan child protection adviser for help and advice. When faced with specific legal concerns, clergy should seek advice from the diocesan registrar or diocesan child protection adviser. Social services and the police can also be approached for guidance without the need to divulge names (see pp. 34–5).

Reflection – confidentiality

- How have you felt when divulging sensitive personal information about yourself to a professional person (for example GP, counsellor or minister)? How did you feel about meeting them again, particularly if this was in another context?

- Are there occasions when you find it difficult to hold confidentiality and, if so, what might be the reasons?
- How do you make boundaries of confidentiality clear to those to whom you offer pastoral care?
- How do you distinguish between information shared with you in friendship and information shared with you as a minister?
- How do you safeguard other people's confidentiality when seeking ministerial advice and support for yourself?
- How would you respond and what action might you take in the following circumstances? What factors would affect your decision?
  - a parishioner discloses that child abuse has taken place in the past, or is currently being perpetrated within their family
  - an allegation of child abuse is made against a parishioner or colleague
  - a child or young person discloses that they have been or are being abused, but does not want their parents, social services or police to be informed
  - a parishioner or colleague tells you that they have abused, or are currently abusing, a child or young person

1.17 Pastoral records

When paper or electronic records are kept the obvious danger is of someone inappropriate gaining access to information, or of its being used in some other context. Clergy should be aware of how the Data Protection Act 1998 applies to pastoral and parish records. Among other things the Act requires that records should not include information about individuals without their consent. Information should be accurate and relevant to its purpose, kept up to date, stored securely and not held longer than necessary. 'Information about an individual's sexual life or the commission or alleged commission of an offence' should not be disclosed to a third party, without the person's explicit consent, except 'in the interests of detecting or preventing crime or when seeking legal advice'. Information identifying a third party (e.g. a victim or informant) should not be disclosed without consent, 'unless disclosure is reasonable in all the circumstances' (House of Bishops 2004).

- If ministers keep notes of pastoral encounters as a reminder to themselves, these should not be identifiable by another person, should be kept securely and destroyed at the earliest opportunity.
- In some circumstances, where there are allegations of abuse, conflict of interest or disciplinary matters, it will be necessary to keep a signed and dated record of events. (For example, a person who is being bullied or abused may need to keep a record of what has been said, in order to seek protection or redress; a minister who has received a disclosure of abuse should keep an accurate written record.) Such records should be made as soon as possible after the event, kept securely and in a way that protects confidentiality.
- Written references should be stored securely.
- Particular care should be taken to safeguard confidentiality when transmitting information electronically.
- Only in exceptional circumstances should personal information be passed on to a colleague or successor and again, only in exceptional circumstances should this be without the consent of the person concerned. Appropriate advice should be sought, for example from the diocesan adviser for child protection and/or from the diocesan registrar before doing so.
- Provision should be made for the appropriate safeguarding or destruction of confidential material in the event of the minster's sudden incapacitating illness, accident or death.

1.18 Telephone answering machines and services

It is important to be clear about who has access to answering machines and who may be present in the room when messages are being recorded or played back. The outgoing message should indicate whether the phone is only for church business or whether it is also for family messages. Answering services which do not identify the recipient's name or number can discourage someone from leaving a message. A message recorded by the minister will always be more welcoming for those who are anxious or in distress than an impersonal recorded voice. A personally recorded message is also a safeguard against someone misdialling and leaving a message on the wrong machine or answering service. Similar safeguards are necessary regarding access to mobile phone, computer and e-mail.

1.19 Preaching, prayer and confidentiality

Ministers also need to be aware that, even when a story is disguised to make it anonymous, for example in preaching, there may still be a real risk of recognition and identification (or misidentification, which can be as damaging), leading to the undermining of trust. Particular care should be taken to seek permission before telling someone else's story, even in disguised form. People's names should not be included in public intercessions or parish publications unless they have given explicit permission.

PROFESSIONAL COUNSELLING

As a specific professional activity, developed in the late twentieth century, counselling is defined as taking place when the counsellor (whether working in a voluntary or paid capacity) reaches an explicit agreement with the person in the role of client, to provide a confidential setting within which he or she can feel safe enough to share difficulties, pain, confusion or despair, in a way which may not be possible with friends or family. Counselling sessions take place away from the client's home, at intervals and for a length of time agreed between counsellor and client. Maintaining and safeguarding the boundaries of time and place are the counsellor's responsibility, and are important in creating a safe and peaceful environment in which the client can explore his or her difficulties. Counselling may involve only two or three sessions or continue over a period of months or years.

In this country there is, at present, no clear distinction between counselling and psychotherapy. Differences relate more to how far the individual psychotherapist or counsellor's training, supervision, skill, self-awareness and experience enable them to work at the emotional and psychological depth appropriate to each individual client.

Relationship

The relationship between the client and the counsellor is an essential part of the process and the complex feelings evoked within this relationship may require sensitive exploration. As trust is built up, the counsellor will encourage the client to look at aspects of his or her life, relationships and self, which he or she may not have considered or felt able to face before. There may be exploration of early relationships, to discover how the client came to react to certain people or situations in ways that contribute to his or her difficulties. Whatever theoretical approaches the counsellor uses, the ultimate aim is the autonomy of the client: for the client to make his or her own choices and decisions and to put them into effect.

Supervision

Exploration of difficult feelings and relationships makes heavy demands on both client and counsellor, and an essential part of any counsellor's training is the development of their self-understanding and self-awareness. In order to be empathic, without becoming over-involved, the counsellor needs to be able to recognize when the client's experience is touching difficulties in their own experience, past or present. They need to develop a heightened capacity to monitor their own inner process, and to be able to recognize and work with the complexity of interpersonal issues which can arise in an 'in-depth' helping relationship, particularly one which continues over an extended period. Regular supervision, in which the counsellor discusses their work and their own feelings and responses in relation to their client, in a confidential setting, is a professional requirement.

Training

A counsellor is someone whose basic skills and attitudes have been specially developed through training, personal therapy and ongoing supervision. It is crucial for clergy to be clear that, if they feel called to engage in ongoing counselling relationships in which deep and intense feelings may arise, then they too require the training in self-awareness and the levels of support which the counselling profession has come to recognize as essential.

Payment

Originally counselling in this country was offered as a service by trained volunteers operating within voluntary agencies which did not charge. Although a limited amount of counselling and psychotherapy is still provided free of charge through the National Health Service and through employee-assistance programmes, voluntary agencies usually invite a donation according to ability to pay and most counselling is now provided by counsellors and therapists in private practice. Payment clearly makes a difference to the relationship between counsellor and the person receiving counselling and would be inappropriate in a relationship of pastoral care.

GOVERNMENT GUIDANCE ON CONFIDENTIALITY IN CHILD PROTECTION:

The law recognizes that disclosure of confidential information without consent or a court order may be justified in the public interest to prevent harm to others. The key factor in deciding whether to disclose confidential information is proportionality: is the proposed disclosure a proportionate response to the need to protect the welfare of the child? The amount of confidential information disclosed, and the number of people to whom it is disclosed, should be no more than is strictly necessary to meet the public interest in protecting the health and well being of a child. The more sensitive the information is, the greater the child-focused need must be to justify disclosure and the greater the need to ensure that only those professionals who have to be informed receive the material. (Department of Health 2003)

If someone believes that a child may be suffering, or be at risk of suffering significant harm, then s/he should always refer his or her concerns to the local authority social services department... While professionals (and others) should seek, in general, to discuss any concerns with the family and, where possible, seek their agreement to making referrals to social services, this should only be done where such discussion and agreement-seeking will not place a child at increased risk of significant harm. (Department of Health 1999)

2

Power, Authority and Vulnerability

*So Jesus called them and said to them, 'You know that among
the Gentiles those whom they recognize as their rulers lord it
over them, and their great ones are tyrants over them. But it is
not so among you; but whoever wishes to become great among
you must be your servant, and whoever wishes to be first
among you must be slave of all. For the Son of Man came not
to be served but to serve, and to give his life a ransom for
many.' Mark 10.42–45*

2.1 Human and divine power

Power in the human context can be defined as 'the ability to
influence the behaviour, thoughts, emotions and attitudes of
other people' (Bons-Storm 1996, p. 25). The power held by
human beings in our society is derived from a variety of sources,
including money and possessions, physical health and strength,
age, gender, colour, ethnic origin, educational attainment and
social status. In a secular context power tends to be seen as something negative, evoking images of control, exploitation and
abuse. Often power is spoken of as if it is a possession in limited
supply which will diminish if shared. Thus power becomes confused with domination, although they are not the same. The Bible
teaches us that power can be used destructively or in ways that
are liberating, enabling others to flourish and grow. Christians
believe that power belongs to God, but that as 'participants in the
divine nature' (2 Peter 1.4) and through the power of the Holy
Spirit, we share in God's power. This life-enhancing power is
crucial in the story of salvation and a key issue in our spiritual
life. We should not hide it or deny it, but own it and use it

36

creatively in the service of others and to build up the whole Church. Jesus, in his life and ministry, shows us divine power being used in response to human need, but always inviting and never forcing a response (Doctrine Commission 2003).

2.2 Inequalities of power in ministerial relationships

All ministers need to recognize and be sensitive to inequalities of power in ministerial relationships and to use their power in ways that are positive and enabling for others. At times this may mean that a minister has to consciously set aside his or her own power in order to empower the other person. Wisdom in the exercise of power can only be achieved through a willingness to examine how we use our power and humility in accepting criticism from those who are less powerful. It also requires that those who feel relatively powerless resist the role of victim and have the courage to confront those who hold power in relation to them. It takes courage to risk offering honest criticism to someone in authority, especially if they are someone we like or whose approval matters to us. It also requires the humility to recognize that sometimes our criticisms may be misjudged or unfair (Doctrine Commission 2003).

The story of the Canaanite woman (who challenges Jesus saying to him 'Yes, Lord, yet even the dogs eat the crumbs that fall from their masters' table', to which he responds 'Woman, great is your faith! Let it be done for you as you wish') exemplifies the creative possibilities when both the powerful and the powerless are able to listen and learn from each other (Matt. 15.21–28). Refusal to listen to another person's point of view comes from a fear of losing power. Jesus' response demonstrates a very different possibility. The Canaanite woman's courage in confronting Jesus and his willingness to listen bring him a wider understanding of his calling, while she is empowered in her faith and her daughter is healed.

2.3 Authority and ordination

Authority is power that is both explicit and legitimate. Clergy need to be aware that, even if they see themselves as sharing power or working collaboratively, ordination confers a particular authority which can be extremely influential upon lay people. Such authority encompasses not only the institutional authority of official appointment, but also the authority from God to be a symbolic representative of the community of faith and religious tradition. This authority is symbolized at ordination with the words, 'Receive this book as a sign of the authority which God has given you this day . . .'

It may be difficult for some who hold the authority of ordained ministry to recognize its effect on others, particularly if they experience themselves as lacking power or influence. Ordained ministers who are insecure in themselves, or feel that their authority is threatened in some way, may compensate by misusing the authority of ordination as if it were their possession. They may rely upon it to bolster their own fragile self-esteem or to enhance their status and power in relation to lay people, rather than seeing it as something to be used to empower the whole faith community.

Ordained ministers need to be particularly aware of how the authority of ordination may affect those whom they are helping. Authority explicitly derived from God will be especially potent in its effect on people of faith. It may make it much harder for them to be critical or to complain, even when there are major failures of ministerial competence or integrity. Authority ascribed to an individual tends to increase the impact that their approval or disapproval, neglect or support has on those who recognize that authority. As a result, the views and opinions of clergy can have a powerful positive or negative influence on parishioners, even though the individual ordained minister might feel that their influence is negligible. It requires humility and imagination to remain in touch with the powerlessness and vulnerability which lay people, junior colleagues or those in training may experience. Their response to feeling powerless may be on a spectrum from uncritical obedience to hostile rejection of authority.

All ministers exercising authority within the Church need to be aware of how authority can be misused or abused, whether consciously or not, and to have constantly in mind their servant status.

2.4 Typology of power

Rollo May's typology of power (1972) can be helpful in assessing the way we exercise power within ministerial relationships where there are inequalities of power:

- *exploitative power* dominates, using force and coercion, such as threats or destructive criticism;
- *manipulative power* controls in more subtle or disguised ways, for example by exclusion from significant communication or using the other person to meet one's need to be needed;
- *competitive power* is deeply ingrained in our culture, particularly in our educational and economic systems. It can be positive and energizing when parties are relatively equal, for example in sport, but is destructive where there is an imbalance of power;
- *nutritive power* sustains and empowers, enabling the less powerful person to develop their own competence and freedom to act, as when adults enable children to do things for themselves, even if to start with they need help and support;
- *integrative power* respects the freedom of the other person and encourages their potential strengths; it involves relating to them as an equal, albeit with a different role, as in a training relationship where the training incumbent brings skills and experience in ministry and the curate brings skills and experience from previous employment such as teaching.

The following questions are important for all in pastoral ministry:

- What forms of power are most appropriate and life-enhancing in the context of pastoral care?
- What forms of power are negative and destructive in their effects?

- Does the minister exercise power over others or use power to enable others?
- How can power be exercised with a care and sensitivity for those who feel less powerful and an awareness of how it feels to be vulnerable and relatively powerless?

The use of exploitative, manipulative or competitive power is always damaging within pastoral relationships. Such approaches to power emphasize inequalities, so that the exercise of power by one person diminishes the power of another. In contrast, both nutritive and integrative forms of power enhance rather than restrict the power of others. Roles may be different but relationship and mutuality are encouraged. Both parties are willing to listen to each other and each is open to the possibility of change. Influence is two-way and power becomes an energy which flows between people, instead of a scarce resource being competed for. It is then a creative and healing resource, enabling both individuals and groups to discover their strengths and to fulfil their potential. Such life-giving energy increases as it is shared, so that the whole faith community can be empowered in the worship and service of God.

Reflection – inequalities of power

- Recall relationships (in both secular and church contexts) where there have been inequalities of power between you and another person. Use Rollo May's typology of power to identify how power was used or responded to by the other person or by you. What did you learn from those experiences about negative and positive uses of power?

2.5 Gender and power in secular society

Historically there have been considerable differences in the ways men and women in our society have exercised power. Although patterns are changing, such differences continue to have a significant, though often unrecognized, influence. In some areas of secular employment, particularly those where women have parity of education and income, women are now established on an equal footing with men. However, women are still less likely to attain the most senior positions in secular society, they still suffer inequalities in pay and pensions and, in general, men continue to hold more social, economic and political power than women.

In secular organizations, where women now hold senior positions, the model for exercising authority still derives from a dominant masculine culture, emphasizing challenge, competitiveness, rationality and targets. Women who adopt this pattern may be criticized for being harsh and aggressive, whereas men who behave in similar ways are more likely to be seen as behaving confidently and positively. Women who do not adopt more typically masculine patterns of behaviour may experience being unheard and invisible, for example by having their ideas either ignored or attributed to male colleagues. In mixed committees, discussion groups or informal social groups it is not uncommon for subject matter to be dominated by men's interests and for women to have difficulty in finding an opening in which to make a contribution. (Of course men may also find themselves marginalized, if they are unable or unwilling to conform to stereotypical patterns of behaviour.)

2.6 Gender and power in the Church

In the Church of England, the ordination of women to the priesthood has brought profound changes in the part that women can play in the leadership of the Church at the local level. However, it is easy to overlook how recently an entirely male priesthood ministered to predominantly female congregations. While the culture of the Church is changing, it still lags behind many of the developments in the secular world and there are relatively few women in those senior positions open to them. At diocesan and national level, church leadership is still predominantly male and, within this masculine world, even the most able and articulate women may find it difficult to have their voices heard.

Many men, ordained and lay, are affirming in their attitude towards the ministry of women and many senior staff encourage individual women clergy. However, they may still be unaware of the underlying structural issues which can disempower women in ministry. Younger women entering ordained ministry in the Church of England, or older women who have experienced the relative gender equality of secular employment, are likely to experience some culture shock as they begin training or enter parish ministry. This may not be obvious to them while things are going well, but it is likely that, when conflict or tensions arise, they will have to deal with attitudes towards women which may seem dated, patronizing, discriminatory and damaging. There are still many church contexts where gender issues cannot be spoken about without arousing bafflement or irritation from both women and men. Women with a vocation to ordained ministry need courage, wisdom and support in discerning when and how to challenge such attitudes.

2.7 Men, women and power

As human beings our similarities will always be greater than our differences. Nevertheless, it is obvious that as boys and girls, women and men, our bodily experience is different and must impact on how we experience each other and the world around us. As research into physiological influences on our behaviour progresses, our understanding of the underlying causes of the different ways in which men and women tend to think, perceive the world and interact will increase.

Amid the varied social contexts of postmodern society it is difficult to generalize about our experiences of power and gender, which are clearly far less rigidly defined than they used to be. Generalizations about gender can always be criticized for failing to honour diversity and individuality, but they may also help us to identify how we are restricted by the culture which has formed us and of which we are a part. While there may be a wide spectrum of experiences, the socialization which a child receives in family, social and school life continues to be affected by gender in ways which will influence interactions in adult life.

Typically boys and men are encouraged to develop confidence in exercising power, reinforcing the greater size and strength of their bodies and encouraging them to feel that it is good to be powerful. The energy and vitality which this familiarity with power brings can be used in creative initiatives and has an important part to play in ministry. However, its downside may be too much emphasis on men feeling they have to be strong and consequent pressure on them to deny feelings of vulnerability and weakness (Hahn 1991). As a result men who are afraid or unable to acknowledge weakness may try to avoid facing their vulnerability by self-harming behaviour such as working too hard, excessive social drinking, or escaping into extra-marital affairs. Or they may succumb to illness and exhaustion through the struggle to maintain a façade of strength and invulnerability.

Girls and women are still more likely to be socialized to be passive and responsive rather than to initiate, a pattern reinforced by the way their bodies teach women to surrender to the processes of life. The positive side of this can be a willingness to wait and trust, to be attentive, allowing and enabling things to happen rather than forcing the pace. There may also be more readiness to live with the emptiness of loss, rather than immediately wanting to fill the space with something new (Hahn 1991).

Traditionally, women have been encouraged to use their power to nurture and develop others' gifts (for example as wives and mothers, or in professions such as teaching, nursing, social work or counselling). The nurturing and integrative use of power has always been (and still is) undervalued by secular society and this has also influenced attitudes towards the exercise of power in the Church. While enabling others to achieve their potential should be a central aim of pastoral ministry for which women's experience equips them well, there is also the risk that women may limit their expectations of themselves and miss opportunities to explore the full extent of their gifts or to use them creatively in the public realm. Women, particularly if they are struggling for recognition of their abilities and potential, may also deny their vulnerability and, like men, they may get into self-harming patterns of overwork, excessive social drinking or extra-marital affairs. However, a woman's pattern of self-harm is more likely to be bound up with damaging feelings of powerlessness and to take place in the privacy of home. Examples might be eating disorders, secret drinking, excessive spending or exhausting herself in trying to fulfil responsibility for cleaning, shopping, cooking and childcare to unrealistic standards, in addition to work outside the home.

2.8 Women's access to power in the public realm

Until relatively recently most women had to rely on indirect access to power in the public realm, usually through their husband's position. As a result, women have been less confident and experienced in using their power to influence events more directly. This has often limited their involvement in decision-making, although organizations such as the Mothers' Union have played an important part in enabling women to find their voice and gain experience in public leadership. The ambivalence women have about being seen as powerful has led many women to underplay their power, using it behind the scenes to influence men or exercising it within the domestic sphere. When women are excluded from the exercise of power in the public domain, or retreat from it because of lack of confidence or fear of rejection, they may develop an exaggerated perception of other people's power. This may reinforce a sense of their own powerlessness and make them more vulnerable to abuse (Hahn 1991).

Women who achieve direct access to power and authority through ordination can find themselves in conflict with women who have relied on informal access to power (for example with the clergy wife who is very involved in her husband's ministry), or with women who have been confined to exercising their power and control in aspects of parish life traditionally allocated to women, such as flower arranging or catering. The ensuing tensions may lead to frustration and hurt. Women who have struggled to have their vocation recognized may feel resented, while a woman who has sacrificed herself for her husband's ministry or has devoted herself to the domestic aspects of parish life may feel threatened. Women in positions of authority still have relatively few role models of women exercising leadership in the Church. They can therefore feel undermined by comments from colleagues and parishioners suggesting that they are 'too powerful', with the implication that this makes them unattractive and unfeminine and threatens their relationships. As a result, lay and ordained women who hold authority within the Church may feel ambivalent about openly exercising their power for fear of criticism or rejection.

When Christian theology challenges the use of power over others and calls for a willingness to be vulnerable and to serve, it may be a very appropriate challenge to more typically masculine ways of exercising power. Although women can also misuse their power, women are usually more attuned than men to using it to nurture and enable others and more in touch with the paradoxical strength of embracing vulnerability (Hahn 1991). However, women may need to be aware of a tendency to manipulate (albeit unconsciously) in situations where they feel powerless. They may have to learn courage in exercising their power and authority in ways that are transparent and unambiguous. Women are also more likely to need a theology which encourages them to be confident in using the full range of their gifts and abilities in Christian ministry. Mary's 'Let it be with me' in response to God's call is a strong and positive affirmation of faith, and the language of the Magnificat speaks of empowerment, not passive acceptance.

2.9 Inequalities of power in pastoral care

Any relationship in which one person seeks help from another involves asymmetrical power and it is crucial that all ministers acknowledge this reality. The 'provider' inevitably holds more power than the person needing help. This inequality increases if the helper has the authority of an official or professional position (e.g. priest, teacher, doctor, police officer, etc.). It is abusive to use such asymmetrical power to gratify needs for affirmation, let alone to manipulate or coerce an individual to satisfy sexual desires or to obtain material or financial advantage.

In pastoral ministry, power and authority will be experienced differently depending on the gender of both the person offering pastoral care and the person receiving that care. The ascribed authority and power of male pastors or senior colleagues will be reinforced by the power still inherent in being a man in our society. Male ministers therefore need to be particularly aware of the possibility of misusing (albeit unconsciously) or abusing this power, particularly when ministering to women or relating to female colleagues in ministry. Male ministers also need to be aware of how easy it is to ignore or override the quieter voices of women. Greater height, bulk, strength and volume of voice can all have a powerful impact and men need to recognize how physical presence may affect others and can be misused to ensure that they are heard and others are not.

In contrast to male colleagues, the power that a woman minister holds, when she exercises leadership or offers pastoral ministry to a parishioner, will be in tension with the comparative lack of power which still underlies the position of women in society and in the Church. The dynamics of power are therefore likely to present a different combination of challenges, risks and opportunities and will impact differently on a woman minister's pastoral care relationships. A woman minister will need to be particularly aware of this when ministering to men and may need to work hard at using her authority effectively, neither denying power nor using it abusively.

Men and women in ministry need a willingness to examine their different experiences of power exercised in pastoral ministry and to learn from each other. Since the ordination of women to the priesthood, women's approach to their ministry, which is often very different from that of men, gives opportunity for both men and women to gain greater self-awareness and deeper insights into the impact of gender on pastoral relationships.

2.10 Dependency in pastoral relationships

The imbalance of power in helping relationships raises issues of dependency. Becoming dependent in adult life, through illness, bereavement, marriage breakdown, redundancy etc., can evoke powerful childhood experiences of helplessness and dependency. If, as children, our dependency needs were met in ways which respected our autonomy and personhood, then as adults we will

probably be able to receive help, without feeling unduly threatened and without becoming over-dependent. We will probably
also be able to offer help without creating undue dependency in
others. However, where our early experiences of dependency
were damaging, we may react in quite extreme ways when we feel
powerless or inadequate in relation to perceived authority figures,
either fighting back to preserve autonomy or retreating into
unquestioning dependency.

It is natural to find satisfaction in ministering to others, and in
pastoral care a phase of dependency may be a vital part of the
healing process. However, there is a risk of needing others to
need us, thereby encouraging inappropriate dependency. Warning signs might be a habitual inability to say 'no' to any request,
or feeling threatened when those we are helping no longer need
us, or begin to seek greater independence and autonomy, or even
to challenge us. Signs of increasing autonomy indicate growth
and need to be recognized and affirmed.

2.11 Projection and power in pastoral relationships

However ethically and sensitively power is exercised, the inequality of power in pastoral relationships may evoke feelings in the
person being helped that derive from childhood relationships
with authority figures and carers, particularly mothers, fathers
and teachers. When this happens the person may feel helpless,
childlike and vulnerable, projecting onto their helper positive,
negative or ambivalent feelings from past relationships, particularly those with parents. They may consequently react as if the
power is being exercised in a dominating, manipulative or competitive way, despite the minister's best efforts to be caring and
helpful. In these circumstances the minister may have to work
extremely hard to understand the dynamics of the relationship
and to sustain it on a positive basis. Likewise the minister may
experience positive or negative feelings towards the person they
are helping, which derive from their own past relationships. (In
psychotherapy these phenomena are known as transference
and countertransference.) Gender will have a powerful influence
on the pattern of such projections. Male clergy may trigger

unresolved father–son/father–daughter issues and female clergy unresolved mother–daughter/mother–son issues. The minister's age in relation to the parishioner's will be an additional factor determining the pattern of these projections. Unresolved issues from sibling relationships may also be brought to the surface. The minister's own unresolved issues from their family of origin may also be opened up and need to be worked through with a supervisor, consultant or counsellor who offers safe distance from the pastoral relationship.

There are potentially positive aspects to the parent–child or sibling feelings evoked in pastoral relationships. Helping relationships, in which the minister responds to trust and vulnerability with respect and compassion, can play a significant part in healing damage from exploitation, deprivation or abuse in past relationships. However, because transference of emotions from parent–child relationships may be present, any coercive behaviour and any transgression of sexual boundaries (regardless of whether the other person appears to consent) are extremely damaging and abusive and will compound childhood (or adult) experiences of abuse.

For this reason, self-awareness, particularly in the area of sexual and emotional needs, is an essential requirement for anyone engaged in any form of pastoral care. We all need to recognize, with humility, that our unmet sexual and emotional needs can distort our judgement.

Reflection – gender and power

- How did you feel as you read the sections on gender and power?
- As a child, was your home predominantly male or female or evenly balanced between the genders? Were boys and girls treated and expected to behave differently?
- How might your childhood experiences influence the way you relate to members of your own or the opposite gender now?

- Are women and men enabled to contribute their gifts in every sphere of your local church, or underrepresented in some areas?
- What differences, if any, do you see in the ways men or women minister and in how people respond to their different approaches to ministry?
- Have you experienced strong negative or positive feelings towards a professional person (doctor, nurse, counsellor, minister) helping you? Have you been aware of a person you were helping having strong negative or positive feelings towards you? How might your feelings and responses in these situations be affected by gender?

2.12 Preaching, prayer and power

Preaching and prayer within the parish arise from the minister's discernment of the spiritual and pastoral needs of the local church community and its individual members. Preaching the Word and prayer in public worship bring great responsibility. Members of the congregation are not in a position to answer back and preaching and prayer can sometimes be used manipulatively or abusively to achieve the minister's own ends, rather than to discern and fulfil the will of God. It can be hard to challenge someone who appears to have greater theological knowledge. It is particularly difficult to challenge someone who claims God's authority for their words and actions or that God has spoken to them in a certain way. However, whether we are ordained or lay, theologically trained or not, discernment of God's will requires us to listen deeply to others as well as to our own inner voice and is rooted in wisdom and humility, not conviction that we are right.

Prayer with an individual can be a vital part of pastoral care but should only be offered, never imposed. It requires sensitivity to the individual's personality and faith tradition. Will this person be disturbed or helped by extempore, silent or more traditional forms of prayer?

When a minister meets with an individual for the first time in a pastoral encounter and deeply personal issues are shared, extempore prayer can be particularly powerful, especially if the person has no previous experience of this way of praying. The minister needs to be aware of this and it may be appropriate to seek permission (e.g., 'How would you feel if we prayed together?') and to remain alert to the impact on the person being prayed for. Praying together can trigger very deep emotions, including tears, and can be a profound spiritual experience. For these very reasons, care needs to be taken never to misuse it to manipulate or coerce the individual towards the minister's point of view.

2.13 Abuse of power

Any misuse of a pastoral relationship is abusive. Such abuse may be emotional, physical, psychological, sexual or spiritual, and it may be covert or blatant. Often it is subtler forms of abuse, particularly emotional abuse, which are the least recognized by either perpetrator or recipient. Abuse within the Church causes incalculable damage to the person abused. Members of the congregation are also likely to feel a profound sense of betrayal when one of their leaders abuses power in some way. Confidence in the Church will almost certainly be undermined and, for some, faith in God may also be irreparably damaged or destroyed.

2.14 Spiritual abuse

Spiritual abuse includes using religious power and authority and the concept of Christian obedience to coerce others into behaviour or matters of belief which they would not freely choose for themselves. Christian discipleship involves sacrifice, but sacrifice is a gift freely given. Assuming that another person will make a sacrifice (e.g. foregoing legitimate working expenses or reasonable time off; expecting someone to take on church responsibilities because their husband or wife is ordained) without offering them a real choice, is a form of theft. Clergy, lay ministers or lay people can all make and be affected by such inappropriate demands for sacrifice, which may also damage spouses and children (House of Bishops 2001). Coercion can take subtle forms and those in more senior positions (such as training roles) need to be aware that, by assuming or expecting someone to do something which they find frightening, disturbing, or which they fear could put their health and safety at risk, they are making it difficult for them to refuse and are depriving them of freedom to choose. Such potentially threatening activities might include expecting someone to appear on the media or lead a high-profile event for which they felt inadequately prepared. It could also be an activity for fundraising or publicity purposes, such as abseiling down a church tower or running a marathon, which could bring a potential health risk.

2.15 Harassment and bullying

The following definitions of racial and sexual harassment and bullying summarize and quote from the House of Bishops' paper, 'The Mistreatment of Adults by those Authorised by Bishop's Licence to Leadership Positions in the Church' (2001).

Racial harassment is verbal or physical behaviour which is offensive or intimidates, humiliates, ridicules or undermines another person because of their colour, race, nationality or ethnic origin.

Sexual harassment can be either a single incident or persistent behaviour and includes any inappropriate or unwanted physical or sexual attention. It could include remarks about appearance which some would find acceptable, but which for another are unwelcome, particularly if they have made it clear that they want them to stop. Sexual harassment also includes:

- insulting, ridiculing or marginalizing someone because of their gender, or sexual orientation
- overfamiliar or suggestive behaviour
- compromising invitations or gifts
- inappropriate touching
- suggestions that sexual favours or submissive behaviour might bring promotion or refusal hinder it.

Bullying can take place in isolation or in front of other people and can include:

- unfair and excessive criticism or criticism in front of others
- ridicule, public insults, shouting, pushing, pinching and physical beating
- repeatedly interfering with someone's possessions
- consistently ignoring a person or their point of view or excluding them by talking only to a third party
- consistently setting unreasonable work targets or unachievable tasks
- withholding information or resources
- removing areas of responsibility without proper explanation or negotiation
- giving individuals menial or trivial tasks
- taking credit for other people's ideas
- persistent negative criticism given without proper supervision or support
- consistently undervaluing a person's efforts without attempts to help them improve performance.

2.16 Responding to harassment and bullying

Any person who is being bullied or harassed is likely to feel disempowered and fearful that they will not be believed. Men or women can bully and harass or be the victim of such behaviour. However, a woman may feel especially vulnerable in making a complaint against a man in a leadership position within the Church, fearing that male solidarity and 'very deep-seated patterns within the Church that protect men and male leadership' will make it harder for her voice to be heard (Jamieson 1997, p. 121). People who bully do not do so in front of those whose power they respect. They may be likeable and pleasant in many other situations and are usually skilful at concealing what is happening, only bullying those they sense are in some way vulnerable. This can create a situation in which a previously self-assured person quickly loses self-esteem and becomes frightened and disorientated. If the bullying persists they will almost always need the support of a third party to hear their story and to help them find the strength to take action against it. Healing and recovery may take a long time and require professional help.

It is crucial that all reports of bullying or harassment are taken seriously by senior staff and not discounted as a clash of personalities. False accusation is a possibility, but the greater risk is that bullying or harassment will continue unchecked. Where bullying has taken place, there need to be safeguards to prevent it happening again to the person who has already been bullied. No other person should be placed in that situation of vulnerability without a full investigation into the validity of any allegations.

2.17 Manipulation and powerlessness

Manipulation can be a way of concealing the exercise of influence, power or control. Most of us dislike the thought that we are being manipulated, or that we might be considered manipulative. However, it is quite normal to manipulate to achieve ends that we feel are important. Often it is simply a matter of presenting things in a way which will bring agreement and avoid unnecessary conflict or confrontation. For much of the time we are unaware of what we are doing or our manipulations are sufficiently subtle or positive in outcome for other people not to notice. More extreme forms of manipulation, particularly when seeking help from another person, are usually a response to feeling powerless and a way of attempting to exercise influence, power or control without being confronted or rejected. It is difficult to challenge manipulation, because it is not out in the open and this can leave the person being manipulated feeling damaged and without a voice (see pp. 71–7).

Individuals who, as children, have learned that manipulation is the only effective way to get their immediate needs met can make enormous demands on those who minister. They usually end up exhausting those who try to help them, while their deeper needs remain unmet. However, simply labelling someone as manipulative does not solve the problem. It may be necessary to confront their behaviour with a combination of understanding and firmness, in order to establish clear boundaries to the pastoral relationship.

Ministers who are insecure in their own authority may have difficulty in using it in ways that allow others the freedom to question or confront appropriately and constructively. All ministers need to examine whether they are using their power and authority to control others in a manner that encourages them to resort to manipulation. It is possible to diminish the feelings of powerlessness in others by:

- sharing information and decision-making
- being willing to recognize and admit to mistakes or to apologize for hurt caused, even when it was unintended
- listening and communicating effectively.

Even mature parishioners (or clergy) will regress to childhood patterns of responding to authority figures if power and authority are used in ways that evoke feelings of powerlessness. It is worth remembering that it is usually when we feel most disempowered and impotent that we become manipulative, aggressive or nasty. When people are enabled to feel that their voice will be heard, they usually treat others better and are able to present their own point of view much more effectively.

2.18 Unequal power and conflict

Inequalities of power heighten the likelihood of conflict, whether that conflict is overt or remains under the surface. Identifying when an individual or group is feeling powerless and unheard is a prerequisite for effective conflict resolution. In church life, conflict often simmers under the surface or erupts in bewildering explosions, sometimes with an intensity which seems disproportionate to the situation and can leave minister and parishioners feeling hurt and confused. This is usually because everyone has been afraid to acknowledge their true feelings, pretending all was well, while anger or resentment festered under the surface.

Enabling people to feel that their voice will be properly heard can help to empower them, as can a willingness to acknowledge any failure to understand their point of view and to apologize where appropriate. Unfortunately, for most of us such an approach seems counter-intuitive. When anxious our inclination is to hold onto our power and to justify our own position, making unacknowledged or continuing conflict more likely. However, when people feel heard they are usually more able to listen to another's point of view, making it more possible to manage the inevitable conflicts of community life without disagreements becoming hurtful or damaging. Nevertheless, strategies to empower those who feel powerless may be blocked if past experiences of abuse prevent them from recognizing what is being offered. In such circumstances building trust can be a slow and painstaking process and may make heavy demands on the minister.

2.19 Unequal power and anger

Anger is a complex emotion, of which fear is often a significant component. Carroll Saussy, in *The Gift of Anger* (1995), defines healthy anger as 'a response to being ignored, trivialized, injured or rejected or as an empathic response to witnessing someone else being ignored, trivialized, injured or rejected'. Anger may be expressed in ways that are life-enhancing and healing or vengeful and destructive. For most people, anger is one of the most difficult emotions to experience or to manage. Expressing anger or being on the receiving end of it can be particularly complex in relationships of unequal power, such as pastoral relationships. Fear of rejection or criticism often inhibits a person from getting angry with a minister, while the minister may also be reluctant to own and express anger, for fear of being perceived as uncaring or even abusive. However, if angry feelings are suppressed without addressing their underlying cause, then the risk is that anger leaks out in passive-aggressive behaviour or erupts at an inappropriate time.

Gender will affect the ways in which anger is experienced and expressed. A woman is more likely to have been socialized to suppress or disguise her anger, so that it may be expressed in tears or describing herself as upset, or even smiling while saying she is angry. Men, on the other hand, may be able to show their anger, but may also use it to conceal times when they feel hurt, vulnerable or afraid. In both instances pastoral care relationships can be undermined by miscommunication and consequent mis-understanding of the true nature of the underlying feelings. Such misunderstandings are a particular risk where the one who offers care and the recipient are of different gender.

The power which ministers hold means that if they express anger destructively (whether this is done overtly or indirectly) it can be very damaging to those on the receiving end. Ministers who find it difficult to recognize and acknowledge their anger may also find it hard to be on the receiving end of another person's anger. Ministers therefore need to learn how to deal effectively with their own anger, in order both to use it construc-tively and to respond well to the anger of others. This may mean spending time with their own angry feelings, expressing them in private in words, with paints, crayons or clay, or finding safe physical outlets, such as banging cushions or digging the garden. Anger which is excessive to the actual situation may be contami-nated by unresolved hurt and anger from the past. Reflecting about angry feelings in a journal, praying them and exploring them within the safety of an appropriate professional relation-ship (e.g. with colleague, counsellor, ministerial supervisor) can bring understanding of the source of the anger. The minister will then need to work out how to respond with integrity, reflecting upon whether their angry feelings need to be expressed or sur-rendered. Ministers who can trust their own anger and learn how to express it in ways that are responsible, creative and life-enhancing, rather than destructive, are much more likely to be able to receive anger from others and to enable others to learn to communicate this uncomfortable emotion in ways that are posi-tive (Saussy 1995).

2.20 Pastoral care of vulnerable minority groups

While Christians believe that all human beings are made in God's image and likeness and are accountable to God, we are all part of social processes which tend to marginalize certain groups of people. Jesus' radical response to the marginalized people of his own day shows us that all are eligible for God's new covenant of inclusive love and that we are challenged to recognize and include the marginalized minority groups of our own day (Doctrine Commission 2003). All ministers, but most especially those who are ordained, need to be sensitive to the power dynamics involved in the pastoral care which they offer to minority groups within the Church. They need to be aware that language is powerful in communicating underlying attitudes of which we are barely conscious. An obvious example in our multiracial society would be the insensitive use of 'black' to denote sinfulness and 'white' to symbolize purity and goodness, in the context of preaching or teaching.

Although it is changing, the profile of the ordained ministry of the Church of England is still predominantly white, male and middle class. Our understanding of pastoral care is shaped within this social context. Unexamined assumptions can make us unaware of how the pastoral care we offer is affected by the social context in which we grew up, were educated and trained. Clergy who have moved from another part of the United Kingdom, or from overseas, or whose social background or church tradition and spirituality are very different from that of their parishioners, may underestimate the impact this has on the way they minister and how they are experienced by their parishioners. Clergy who minister to members of minority ethnic groups have a particular responsibility to learn about cultural differences that may affect how pastoral care is perceived and received (Lartey 2003).

At an institutional level, legal requirements have made us increasingly aware of the need for a positive and enabling approach in respect of people with disabilities. However, we can still overlook the needs of individuals whose disabilities are not obvious to us, for example by failing to check that we can be heard properly or assuming that everyone can read with ease. In our anxiety about the Church's failure to attract younger members, we may also forget that in speaking negatively about the older-age profile of a particular church, or through implicitly disparaging references to elderly people, we can convey that older people are somehow of less worth to the Church than younger members of the congregation. Similarly, we may marginalize young people by attitudes and language that fail to welcome and include them.

2.21 Pastoral care of gay, lesbian and bisexual people

One of the most difficult aspects of the Church's debates and divisions over the morality and politics of homosexuality is that the pastoral care of homosexual people and their families can easily be undermined. Ministers need to be aware of the negative impact of this on the significant minority of Christians who are of a gay, lesbian or bisexual orientation, and likely to feel increasingly marginalized. There is no consensus about the social or genetic factors involved in the construction of sexual identity and orientation, but we know that for a substantial minority of people their sexual orientation is towards members of their own sex. It is an inherent aspect of their identity which cannot be changed. While there are some rare examples of people who claim 'healing' and a change in their orientation, for the majority sexual orientation is unchosen and unchanging. It is therefore inappropriate and damaging to try to persuade a person that they can or should attempt to change their sexual orientation. Pastoral care must always relate to the reality of each person's identity as made and loved by God. It requires of the minister an acceptance of the reality of each person's self-understanding.

For some people, particularly older people influenced by the long and powerful tradition of opposition to homosexual practice in society and in the Church, the realization of homosexual orientation in themselves is experienced as a burden. They are likely to have kept their sexual orientation secret and may have attempted to deny or change their orientation, sometimes with damaging consequences for themselves and for their personal relationships. Or they may feel that they are called by God to a life of celibacy, even though this is contrary to their own preferences and may create struggles of faith as well as of sexual identity. Others may find themselves caught up in transient sexual encounters, bringing the risk of health problems and feelings of self-rejection and guilt. For all these people there may be pressure to keep silent about their sexual orientation thereby deepening their sense of personal isolation.

However, an increasing number of homosexual people within and outside the Church are finding the freedom to be more open about their situation. Increasing acceptance of homosexual people and practice in secular society in the past three decades has meant that more gay and lesbian people, including Christians, are entering into publicly acknowledged long-term relationships with people of the same sex. The legal recognition of civil partnerships will increase this trend. For some Christians the decision to enter into a sexual relationship with a member of the same sex brings a major rethinking of their inherited faith and moral viewpoints. For many it has proved to be a liberating and healing experience in which they experience themselves as blessed by God.

A minister's response to such situations will be determined to some extent by their own understanding of the Christian tradition, but it is always important to distinguish between the minister's own moral judgement of another's behaviour and that person's personal story, personal needs and their civil rights as a member of society. All of us, regardless of our sexual orientation, need to be enabled to love and accept ourselves and to experience the unconditional love of God, mediated through the love of our fellow Christians. A minister who believes that homosexual orientation necessitates a calling to celibacy still needs to be pastorally sensitive to the reality of the homosexual person's journey of life and faith, and willing to engage with the truth of their experience. Ministers also need to be sensitive to the pastoral needs of the parents, children and siblings of gay, lesbian and bisexual people, who can also feel very isolated and alienated. All ministers need to recognize the immense damage that can be done by negative or rejecting pastoral responses or thoughtless comments. All expressions of homophobia, the emotional rejection of homosexual people, are completely unacceptable in the Christian Church and should be challenged. Similar awareness is required when caring for people experiencing transgender issues.

Reflection – abuse, manipulation, conflict; diversity and vulnerability

- If you have experienced or witnessed abuse or misuse of power, bullying or harassment within your church, were you able to tell anyone about it? If so, what action was taken to support you or remedy the situation?

- How do you use manipulation to achieve outcomes and avoid conflict in everyday situations with family, friends, parishioners and colleagues?
- How do you react when you sense that you are being manipulated?
- Do you usually avoid conflict or work to bring it into the open so that it can be resolved?
- How aware are you of your own angry feelings? Do you usually express, disguise or suppress them? How do you react to the anger of another person?
- How do inequalities of power affect your responses to the expression of conflict or anger?
- How diverse is your church congregation in gender, age, disability, social, racial, educational, cultural and spiritual backgrounds? How far does this reflect the local community in which the church is situated?
- Who are the members of vulnerable minority groups within your church or local community? How do you ensure that their views are heard and that the church community learns from and affirms them?

2.22 The challenge of training relationships

Clergy have considerable independence in their work. Even where there are ministry teams, clergy get very used to being autonomous and to making many day-to-day decisions about their work without the need to consult with or to inform anyone else. However, training a curate means relinquishing much of that autonomy, often meeting several times a week over a period of three to four years, learning to pray and work together, to establish and maintain good two-way communication, to share aspects of leadership and to be open about strengths and weaknesses. The training incumbent may feel anxious about their ministry being exposed to the scrutiny of the curate, or protective towards areas of work or relationships within the parish which could be unsettled by the arrival of a new minister. The curate, who may live in the same parish as the training incumbent, or in another within the benefice, will be crucially dependent on the training incumbent for guidance, support and encouragement. The match of personalities and expectations may mean that the training relationship gets off to a good start and works well. However, while working together can be creative and rewarding, it is usually a costly process. Both training incumbent and curate have to be ready to make a major commitment of time and energy to build and sustain an effective training relationship. If the relationship does not work well then it will cause frustration and disappointment to one or both parties. If it breaks down then there is almost always immense pain, unhappiness and sense of failure for curate, training incumbent and parishioners, but it is the curate (and his or her family) who are the most vulnerable when this happens.

2.23 Pastoral training

Partners in a training relationship share two tasks in pastoral ministry. First, the pastoral care of parishioners, and, second, the development of the trainee minister's skill and understanding in pastoral care. These tasks raise the issue of appropriate balance between caring for the parishioner and seeking opportunities for training in skills and good practice. There is also the question of whether the parishioner's permission should be sought before they are 'trained upon'.

Clarity about roles, responsibilities and communication and a willingness to explore different perceptions of the pastoral role are all important. As with all shared ministry, there also needs to be discussion about degrees of openness, loyalty and boundaries of confidentiality and an understanding of how projections from and to parishioners may impact on the training relationship. For example, a minister in training may absorb projected feelings of anger or frustration from a parishioner towards their training incumbent and may need to guard against playing these feelings out in the training relationship.

2.24 Power and the training relationship

The training incumbent needs to be aware of the inequality of power and authority implicit in the relationship between trainer and trainee, and should encourage shared exploration of how this may be affecting their working relationship. Given the sensitive nature of pastoral ministry and the crucial importance of the training relationship during the first few years of ministry, meetings with an outside consultant in a neutral position, on something like a quarterly basis, is advisable in order to maintain an effective training relationship. A male training incumbent needs to be particularly sensitive to power issues in working with a female curate and to recognize that gender has a profound effect on approaches to and styles of ministry. A female training incumbent and male curate will also be affected by the gender power dynamic, because the power and authority of the female training incumbent's role is in tension with the less powerful position of women in society.

Both curate and training incumbent may exercise power in any of the ways listed in the typology of power (2.4). Exploitative power and manipulative power are, of course, completely inappropriate in the training relationship. Competitive power is also inappropriate but, given that it is so embedded in our culture, even colleagues who work well together are quite likely to experience some competitive feelings. A training incumbent therefore needs to be secure in their own style of ministry and to have grace to affirm gifts and skills in the curate that they as incumbent do not have. Nutritive power, which sustains, encourages and empowers, will enable the curate to develop new skills and confidence and is especially appropriate early on in the training relationship. Integrative power is also vital, particularly as the relationship progresses. The integrative use of power means establishing a relationship of increasing mutuality as each training partner brings their own unique constellation of gifts, experience, competence and personal style to ministry. This can only happen if both training incumbent and curate develop their ability to give and receive useful and accurate feedback to one another, graciously and without being defensive or negative.

2.25 The training incumbent's spouse and the training relationship

If the training incumbent's spouse is ministering in the training parish or benefice, dual relationships (3.5) can give rise to complex boundary issues. If the spouse is ordained, a reader, lay leader or member of the PCC, both incumbent and spouse need to be particularly aware of the power they hold as a couple in relation to the curate and the curate's spouse. In such circumstances the training incumbent's spouse may intend to relate to the curate as a peer colleague in ministry, and may have a contribution to make to the curate's learning. However, the curate (and spouse) may perceive him or her as exercising informal power and influence through being married to the incumbent. People's perceptions are their reality so that, whatever the actual situation, such perceptions can have a powerful effect on the training relationship. If parishioners share the perception, or if there are pre-existing difficulties in the three-way relationship between training incumbent, spouse and parishioners, this may also impact negatively on the training relationship. (For example, it is not uncommon for difficulties between training incumbent and parish to be projected onto the incumbent's spouse; the curate needs to be sensitive to this and aware of the risk of getting caught up in it.)

Boundaries of confidentiality and responsibility are likely to be complex wherever the training incumbent's spouse is actively involved in leadership in the parish. These boundaries will need sensitive management and good communication by all concerned. They should be discussed and agreed by curate and training incumbent at the start of their relationship and reviewed on a regular basis. Both spouses also need to have a clear understanding of the boundaries and to be in agreement with them. The following issues may arise and need to be addressed:

- the curate may feel that he or she is relating to the training incumbent's marriage rather than to the training incumbent
- a single curate relating to training incumbent and spouse may feel at a disadvantage
- the curate's spouse may feel on the outside of a three-way

relationship (between curate, training incumbent, incumbent's spouse), which affects them through their spouse, but in which they have no voice

- the training incumbent's spouse may feel on the outside of the training relationship and excluded from areas of ministry in which they previously had a voice
- the training incumbent may feel that he or she is relating to the curate's marriage rather than to the curate.

Relationships can become even more complex if the curate's spouse also has a recognized ministry (e.g. as a reader), is an ordinand or has been actively involved in ministry in their former parish. It may be very difficult for the curate's spouse to find a fulfilling role in the parish where their spouse is in training; he or she may feel very uncertain about how much to be involved and wonder if there is a place for them. All concerned will need great sensitivity and a willingness to be transparent about hopes and fears, about difficulties that arise and about how decisions are made.

2.26 The training incumbent's children and the curate's children

The children of the training incumbent and of the curate may be involved together in church or church-related activities or attend the same school. If they get on well together this can be enriching for everybody. However, complex boundary issues can arise when the children of curate and training incumbent attend the same school, particularly if it is a school where one or both clergy take assemblies and/or are involved as governors. It is a good strategy for both sets of parents to agree in advance how they will respond if there are disagreements or upsets between their children, whether at school, at church or in the wider community. The parents also need to be aware that these could arise, if the children pick up tensions between the two sets of parents (a probability at some time in a three- to four-year curacy) and act them out in hostility towards each other. Any difficulties need to be dealt with in a way which does not damage the children, leave either spouse feeling without a voice in relation to their children or undermine the training relationship.

2.27 Integrating the curate into the parish

Often neither the training incumbent and their spouse nor the curate and their spouse are prepared for the complex inter-family relationships they will have to maintain over a period of three or four years. In many parishes there is a complex network of relationships between families and individuals, including the families of ordained clergy. In multi-parish benefices there may also be complex inter-parish networks. Introducing a new curate into this situation (particularly one who is married and/or has children) will impact on the training incumbent's family and the network of parish relationships. The process of integrating the curate and his or her spouse and children into this parish network may be more complex:

- if they are moving in immediately after a previous curate and family have left the parish (particularly if the previous curacy was either problematic or especially positive)
- if relationships in the parish are still settling down after the recent arrival of the training incumbent (particularly if their predecessor's incumbency was either problematic or especially successful)
- if there are other ordained colleagues in the ministry team, whether they are stipendiary, non-stipendiary or retired
- if there is an ordained local minister, particularly one who is still in training, who may feel threatened by the arrival of a curate bringing new ideas, skills and experiences.
- if benefice boundaries have recently been altered, affecting inter-parish relationships.

Such factors need to be taken into account in deciding on the placement of curates and in preparing parish and ministry team for their arrival.

The upheavals and insecurities which many stipendiary curates and members of their families experience during the training years prior to ordination may make it harder for them to integrate within the new parish. For most people, settling into a new home and occupation takes at least two years. The curate, their spouse and family know that before long they will be facing the uncertainties of finding a new job and moving on once more. It can be very difficult for them to keep building new relationships when they know that, after three or four years, they will have to say goodbye and begin again. The pressures on the curate's family will be increased if the upheavals of training have coincided with family transitions, such as children leaving home or parents becoming ill, frail or dying. Sometimes an individual family member or a particular family relationship will be especially vulnerable during the transition period, although their difficulties may be a symptom of the stress on the whole family.

Non-stipendiary ordinands and curates who have to move away from their home parish during training or after ordination may also find it harder to integrate into their training parish if the move means that they are no longer able to worship in the same church as other members of their family. Ordinands used to being able to worship with their families are often inadequately prepared for the pain and loss they will all feel at having to worship separately, whether in a different parish or benefice, or in the same building but no longer together in the congregation.

The curate whose family is finding it hard to adjust to life in the parish or local community can feel burdened by guilt at having uprooted them and deprived them of valued social networks. The curate may also get anxious if tensions arise in their relationship with their training incumbent or with parishioners and be afraid to confront the difficulties in case it makes the situation worse or leads to the curacy breaking down. The curate's spouse and family may feel understandable anger and resentment towards the Church at the upheaval imposed upon them and may project their distress onto the incumbent, the incumbent's spouse or children, or onto the parish. The training incumbent, who may also feel unsure in their role, needs to anticipate and allow for the vulnerability and powerlessness which the curate and their family may experience throughout the curacy.

2.28 Senior staff, authority and power

Clergy in the Church of England are under obedience. They have made public oaths of allegiance and loyalty, and entered the ministry of a Church with a defined structure of authority. The Church of England is part of the 'One Holy Catholic and Apostolic Church' of which the bishops are a sign. Ordination vows, Bishop's Regulations, and the Canons of the Church of England, all form a backdrop to the freedom that ministers exercise in their work.

Decision-making power in the Church of England is distributed in very complex ways, among office holders and bureaucrats, both ordained and lay, bringing the risk of confusion about who has access to power and a tendency for power to be exercised in ways that are not easily scrutinized. No one, whatever their status, is exempt from making mistakes in the exercise of power, and rigorous self-examination and a willingness to accept criticism from others are essential to the properly disciplined exercise of power by senior staff. This does not mean that those who criticize senior staff are always right. They too have a duty of self-examination and a responsibility to seek to offer criticism in ways that are constructive (Doctrine Commission 2003).

Senior ministers fall under the same constraints as all ministers, both with regard to living the gospel life and exercising leadership and pastoral care in ways that carry the respect of their colleagues at local level. Listening, consulting, good communication, clarity about boundaries and confidentiality are part of all ministry, whether parish, sector or senior. All need to hold before themselves a common pattern of pastoral care, ministerial integrity and appropriate conduct.

In an atmosphere of increasing informality, senior staff, including bishops, archdeacons and cathedral deans, may underestimate how their authority heightens the positive or negative impact of their response when clergy or laity seek their advice or support. The effect of criticism, affirmation or perceived indifference will all be intensified. Delay in responding to a letter or answering a phone call or e-mail may be due to pressure of work, but is easily interpreted as lack of care or interest by someone who already feels vulnerable and relatively powerless.

Communication through secretaries or bishop's chaplain, rather than directly, is an inevitable consequence of the administrative pressures on bishops and other senior staff, but can also bring a sense of distance if combined with delay in obtaining a face-to-face meeting. Membership of national secular and church bodies adds to an already heavy load of diocesan responsibilities on senior staff and can also distance senior staff from the everyday pressures of parish ministry.

Diocesan bishops occupy a role which carries the weight of history and has a powerful symbolic importance in representing spiritual authority and the unity of the Church. Tradition and expectation can place a particularly heavy burden on diocesan bishops in some older dioceses, where for centuries their role has been enmeshed in secular class and power structures. Bishops continue to be set apart by differences of dress and by the way they are addressed, emphasizing the significance of their role in local and national church life. These customs of title and dress may encourage clergy and laity to relate to the role rather than to the person within the role. They can also make it harder for bishops to stay in touch with their vulnerable humanity or to be seen and accepted as ordinary human beings.

While senior staff will wish to be pastorally sensitive to ministers who are in difficulty, their responsibility to parishioners and to the wider Church mean that, on rare occasions, they may need to exercise discipline. This is less likely to be necessary where a relationship of trust and honest sharing has been established between ministers and senior staff, and where ministers are known to be acting responsibly in addressing their difficulties, with professional help if appropriate.

2.29 Pastoral care of senior staff

Senior staff also have pastoral needs and face times of personal difficulty or excessive ministerial pressures. It can be particularly hard for them to know whom to turn to for support. They too need to establish support systems that sustain their ministry. If such support is inadequate, then it is likely the pastoral care they offer will be affected. Senior staff and their spouses who have enjoyed parish ministry often miss the sense of belonging to a local Christian community and, in consequence, their ministry may feel lonely and isolated, especially in the first few years. The hierarchical pattern of authority relationships in the Church can make it difficult to establish a mutuality of pastoral care between senior staff and parish clergy. In consequence, parish clergy may be hesitant about expressing pastoral concern for their bishops and archdeacons. They may not recognize how much senior staff also need pastoral support or can be helped by a sensitively offered acknowledgement that they may be experiencing difficulties in ministry and personal life.

Reflection – training relationships, parish and family; senior staff

- What is your experience of how power is used and inequalities of power managed in training relationships in the church and in secular contexts?
- If you are an incumbent, what impact might the arrival of a new curate and his or her family have on (a) your personal relationships, (b) the existing network of parish relationships, (c) ordained colleagues, (d) key lay people?
- If you are an ordinand or curate, how has your vocation to ordained ministry and your training affected your spouse and children or other close personal relationships?
- If you hold a senior position in the diocese, how do you feel about the power and authority your role gives you? Where do you look for ministerial support and is this sufficient?

2.30 Jesus, power and vulnerability

Celia Hahn, in her book *Sexual Paradox* (1991), explores how we all live in the tension between power and vulnerability and how this has a profound effect on pastoral ministry. It is in the nature of our humanity that at times we feel strong and effective and at other times weak and helpless. When we fear or deny our own potential to be vulnerable we are in danger of misusing our power to abuse others. When we deny or lose touch with our power, we may exaggerate the power of others and risk becoming victims of abuse.

Ordained ministers do not hold Godlike qualities which enable them to solve all problems, give them infinite wisdom or preserve them from temptation. However, sometimes those who hold power and authority within the Church (especially in the context of a dominant secular culture in which the Church can seem weak and in decline) may be tempted to appear invulnerable or to succumb to the myth that clergy are somehow a race apart. If clergy act as if they are, then they deny themselves the support we all need. They may also encourage parishioners in an unhealthy dependence on them instead of on God and will eventually be exhausted by the demands they are thereby inviting others to make upon them. The challenge is to work to empower people who, though they may sometimes wish to be helpless and dependent, are also called to be empowered by God.

We see in the life and ministry of Jesus that he lived in this tension between power and vulnerability, and we are called to do the same. Jesus came to earth as a defenceless baby and died in helpless agony on the cross. In his vulnerability he invites us to acknowledge our vulnerability. 'God chose what is weak in the world to shame the strong' (1.Cor. 1.27). Yet in his ministry Jesus also used his power in ways that were challenging and liberating for others. As well as confronting those who held established power, Jesus challenged those who felt themselves to be without power, telling them 'your faith has made you well' (Luke 17.19) and promising the disciples that they would receive the power of the Holy Spirit. So Jesus challenges us to recognize that through faith we have the power to nurture and enable others and to find wholeness in our own lives, pointing us always to God as the source of that power. As he invited his followers, so Jesus invites us to own and share power, demonstrating in his life and ministry that this is a power to be used always with humility and in the service of love, exemplified in the washing of the disciples' feet at the Last Supper (John 13.3–17).

DRAMA AND WINNER'S TRIANGLES

The Drama Triangle (Karpman 1968), derived from Transactional Analysis (Berne 1968), can help identify negative patterns in relationships of unequal power. It describes what happens when people get locked into unhelpful or potentially destructive patterns of relating known as 'games'. When caught up in a Drama Triangle people are likely to feel misunderstood, angry and confused and to get into blaming one another or themselves. The way out of a Drama Triangle is for at least one player to give up trying to change the other players' behaviour and to focus on changing their own. Acey Choy's article 'The Winner's Triangle' (1990), summarized and quoted from here, offers a model for the changes in attitudes and behaviour which enable this shift from Drama to Winner's Triangle.

Drama Triangle

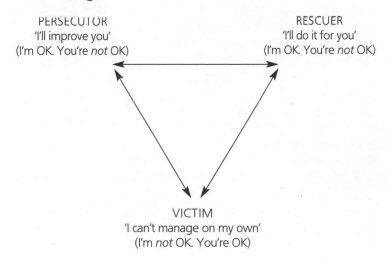

PERSECUTOR
'I'll improve you'
(I'm OK. You're *not* OK)

RESCUER
'I'll do it for you'
(I'm OK. You're *not* OK)

VICTIM
'I can't manage on my own'
(I'm *not* OK. You're OK)

A Drama Triangle may develop when a third party intervenes (i.e. 'rescues') in a relationship difficulty between two individuals (e.g. husband and wife, parent and child), or an individual and an issue in their life (e.g. alcohol misuse, gambling, eating disorder, work addiction).

The person who attempts to 'rescue' is powerless to sort out the difficulty. We can only change our own behaviour. We cannot change someone else's behaviour. If the Rescuer keeps trying to sort out the difficulty, they will become increasingly stressed. They may eventually become either Persecutor (they get so frustrated with the situation that they become punitive) or Victim (they give so much in terms of support that their own life and relationships suffer). Christians sometimes find it hard to recognize when they are getting caught up in this kind of 'game', especially when attempting to offer Christian love, help and support to others.

Positions in the Drama Triangle

Victim

Victims act as if they do not have the resources to solve their problems. (At times of genuine emergency this may be true.) In Drama Triangles the Victim has the resources to solve the problem or to seek skilled help in confronting their difficulties, but resists doing so. Victims do not use clear thinking and problem-solving skills. They allow their feelings to over-whelm them, discounting their ability to think and feel at the same time.

Rescuer

Most Rescuers are genuinely concerned about the Victim's plight, but take over responsibility for thinking and problem-solving. They discount the Victim's ability to assess the situation, take appropriate action and ask for help if needed. Rescuers often do something they do not want to do or more than their share. Rescuing involves taking too much responsibility for another person or their situation and often leads the rescuer to neglect their own needs.

Persecutor

Persecutors are absorbed in satisfying their own needs and acting in their own interests. (We all need to be able to do this to survive in life, but not in ways that disregard others.) They disregard other people's feelings and cause them inconvenience or suffering. They may actively use their energy to get their needs met at the expense of others (active

Persecutors). They may do things badly or neglect things they have undertaken in a way that causes suffering and ignores others' feelings (passive Persecutors). They may have a need to punish and experience triumph over others (retaliatory Persecutors).

Role switches in the Drama Triangle

Individuals may switch roles in a Drama Triangle, without recognizing what they are doing. For example:

- Rescuers get tired of giving out and not getting their own needs met and start to feel Victims. Or they persecute the Victim with impatience, too much good advice or by withdrawing suddenly from the situation. Alternatively, if the Victim finds their way out of the Drama Triangle, the Rescuer may feel threatened and start to behave punitively to get them back in.

- Victims become more and more demanding, in effect persecuting the Rescuer for failing them.

- Persecutors move into rescuing because they feel guilty for behaving badly. Alternatively, they become Victim, as people retaliate or avoid them.

Shifting from Drama Triangle to Winner's Triangle

The way out of a Drama Triangle is to relate to the other players as if they are capable of taking responsibility for their own difficulties. This may trigger strong resistance. Often their behaviour gets worse, as they attempt to restore the status quo. If a Drama Triangle is well established, the person working to break the cycle, from whichever position, may need to consult someone outside in order to clarify what is happening and to maintain their own changes in behaviour. However, with perseverance, new patterns of behaviour can emerge.

Winner's Triangle

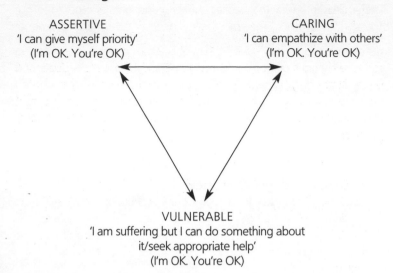

ASSERTIVE
'I can give myself priority'
(I'm OK. You're OK)

CARING
'I can empathize with others'
(I'm OK. You're OK)

VULNERABLE
'I am suffering but I can do something about
it/seek appropriate help'
(I'm OK. You're OK)

Vulnerable position in the Winner's Triangle (alternative to Victim)

Like Victims, vulnerable people realize they are suffering, or have a problem. However, unlike Victims, they know that they can think and feel at the same time. They engage in adult logic and problem-solving, but can also tune in to their feelings. As part of their problem-solving they are willing to ask for appropriate help, resources and support.

Caring position in the Winner's Triangle (alternative to Rescuer)

Caring people, like Rescuers, are motivated by concern for the vulnerable person, but respect the vulnerable person's ability to think, problem-solve and ask for what they want. Caring people do not take over unless asked and unless they really want to. They may then offer to assist in a particular capacity, but are able to stay in touch with their own needs and feelings and to resist pressure to do things they do not want to do. They are able to decide when to be available and to decline without guilt. The most effective way to be usefully available to a vulnerable person, without rescuing, is to offer empathic listening.

Assertive position in the Winner's Triangle (alternative to Persecutor)

Assertive people, like active Persecutors, use their energy to get their own needs met and to stick up for their rights. They recognize that making assertive changes can cause distress to people whose plans depended on the status quo, but, unlike Persecutors, they have no interest in using their energy to punish or bully. While they may use negotiation as part of the problem-solving process, they do not rescue the sufferer by 'fudging' to soften the blow.

From Drama to Winner's Triangle

The following self-beliefs and attitudes support the shift from Drama to Winner's Triangle positions (Choy 1990):

Vulnerable

- I recognize my suffering
- I can solve my problems
- I have the resources myself or can find appropriate help
- I can feel and think at the same time
- I can tune in to my feelings and work out what they are telling me
- I can assess the situation and what I need to do next
- I can protect myself
- My ideas are OK.

Caring

- I can empathize with others but be aware of my own needs and wants
- I can feel OK even when I am not doing things for others
- I can decide how much I'm willing to do, without feeling put upon
- I can find out what people want before taking action on their behalf
- I can allow and enable the other person to do their own thinking and deciding
- I can give myself priority when appropriate.

Assertive

- I can get my needs met and stand up for myself, while respecting and valuing other people's feelings, opinions and thoughts
- I can feel OK without having to get my own back
- I can change things for the better
- I can tolerate causing others discomfort, but do not want to put them down or get my own back
- Others have the right to do things their way, or not do them at all
- There is usually more than one good way to solve a problem.

Default positions in the Drama Triangle

Although another person's behaviour can push us into any one of the positions in the Drama Triangle, most of us tend towards one or two of the positions. These 'default positions' are the product of personal history, social conditioning, social structures and context (e.g. women are more likely to be Rescuers and Victims, avoiding Persecutor role; men are more likely to be Rescuers or Persecutors, avoiding Victim role). The roles we avoid in the Drama Triangle often show us which position in the Winner's Triangle we need to work at most. For example:

- if we avoid any risk of being Victim we may need to learn how to own our vulnerability
- if we avoid any risk of being seen as Persecutor, we may need to learn to be more assertive and in touch with our strengths
- if we always avoid being Rescuer, we may need to find ways to help and enable others, but without disempowering them.

Organizations and the Drama Triangle

Drama Triangles tend to arise in situations where there are real or perceived inequalities of power. They often occur in institutions and organizations with hierarchical power structures and an emphasis on uncritical obedience. They may develop within helping relationships and in helping organizations such as the NHS and Social Services. The Drama and Winner's Triangles can help identify and shift pastoral care or training relationships which have become stuck in unhelpful and repetitive patterns.

Drama and Winner's Triangles and the Gospels

Although the Drama and Winner's Triangles are secular models, they can be tested through examination of Jesus' behaviour in the gospel narratives. Jesus was the master of avoiding being negatively 'triangled' into situations. He did not behave as a Rescuer, a Persecutor or a Victim, but allowed people to make their own choices, without ever attempting to control or manipulate them. He was able to own his own vulnerability, to be compassionate or assertive, without damaging the autonomy of others.

3

Boundaries in Pastoral Care

Keep watch over yourselves and over all the flock, of which the
Holy Spirit has made you overseers, to shepherd the church of
God that he obtained with the blood of his own Son.

Acts 20.28

3.1 Boundaries and Jesus' ministry

Boundaries are an essential safeguard in our relationships with other people, enabling us to respect and protect our own and other people's personal autonomy and space. In the Gospels we see Jesus responding in varied pastoral situations with compassionate respect for the boundaries of others and clarity about his own personal boundaries. For example, Jesus offers the rich young man a clear choice of what he must do to inherit eternal life, loving him and respecting his autonomy, even when he fails the challenge and turns away (Mark 10.17–27).

Boundaries in our relationships also enable us to be clear about what is our responsibility and to resist taking on responsibilities that belong to the other person. Jesus gave unstintingly of his time and energy, but also challenged those who sought healing to take responsibility for their own part in enabling it to happen. Jesus asked blind Bartimaeus to tell him what he wanted him to do, then told him that his faith had made him well (Mark 10.46–52). At the pool of Bethzatha he asked the man who had been ill for 38 years if he wanted to be made well and then challenged him to have faith and stand up and walk, instead of relying on others to bring him to healing (John 5.1–9).

Awareness of personal boundaries can protect ministers from succumbing to unrealistic demands or being overwhelmed by

78

expectations projected onto them because of their role. Boundaries also protect the minister who is too tired or unwell to respond effectively and could put him- or herself and others at risk. Jesus recognized when he was too tired to give any more and went to a deserted place early in the morning, while it was still dark, to find solitude and pray (Mark 1.35). He slept during a time of crisis when, to the consternation of his disciples, waves were swamping their boat, and challenged them for their lack of faith (Mark 4.37–41).

3.2 Discernment in responding

Jesus discerned when to respond immediately and when to wait, showing how an immediate response to a need is not always the same thing as the most effective response. He responded at once to the illness of Simon's mother-in-law (Mark 1.29–31) but allowed the outcast woman with a haemorrhage to delay his response to Jairus, leader of the synagogue (Mark 5.21–43). He also chose to delay when he heard from Mary and Martha that his friend Lazarus was ill (John 11.1–6). On these occasions delay led to a testing and deepening of faith for those who were open to God's resurrection power in their lives.

On occasions when discerning how to respond is difficult, responding at once can seem the easier option. Some people are naturally more intuitive and skilful at discerning the real need underlying a request for help, but accurate intuition requires both sensitivity and self-awareness and can be impaired, especially when the minister is tired, stressed or unwell. Deep levels of discernment in complex pastoral situations require a continuing discipline of prayer, silence, sacrament, Bible study, reflection, rest and a willingness to listen and learn by example. Most ministers will recognize with regret times when, because they were too busy, too preoccupied or too tired, they did not listen to the promptings of the Holy Spirit to guide their response, whether to act immediately or to wait.

Careless delay is never an option and sometimes it is important to seize the moment and respond. However, a person who seeks help does not always need to be seen at once and it is not always helpful to respond instantly to requests, however insistent, unless the need is clearly and objectively urgent. A brief assessment of urgency and the reassurance of a time in the near future when the person will receive undivided, quality attention may enable them to find the inner strength to carry on. They may also gain fresh insights in the intervening time and even discover for themselves a deeper faith in God. The minister will also be able to offer more effective and appropriate help, if not distracted by other duties and demands.

3.3 Responsibility for boundaries

In the past, boundaries in pastoral relationships were more clearly symbolized and communicated by language, dress and behaviour: using titles rather than Christian names, dressing formally, avoiding all but the most formal physical contact, meeting in formalized or chaperoned situations. Nowadays values and behaviours have changed and norms of social contact are much more relaxed and informal. There are many positive aspects to this, but there is also the risk of ambiguity, misinterpretation and manipulation. There has to be greater reliance on the minister's internal emotional and psychological stability and boundaries. Self-awareness is essential to enable him or her to identify when there is a risk of personal or ethical boundaries being broken.

Much pastoral care is by nature flexible, spontaneous and involves creating or responding to opportunities for encounter that are informal and to some extent unpredictable (1.2). Pastoral contacts are not clearly defined and can extend to many different contexts, such as Sunday worship, PCC meetings, prayer and Bible study groups or unexpected encounters in the community. They will often include relationships with the person's family or friends and happen in situations where the minister has little control over the immediate environment. There may be interruptions and distractions, particularly if they take place in the parishioner's home or in a public context. The boundary issues faced by ministers are therefore much more complex and challenging than for counsellors, for whom boundaries are symbolized by appointment time, duration and place of meeting and supported by a framework of ethics and good practice. Despite the complexities they face, ministers usually receive comparatively little training or support in learning the self-awareness and skills necessary to safeguard boundaries (see pp. 32–4).

The minister, not the parishioner, is responsible for setting, communicating and maintaining boundaries in pastoral relationships. It is the minister's responsibility to take care about time, frequency and place of meeting. Even when it is appropriate to negotiate certain aspects of such boundaries, the minister carries primary responsibility for ensuring boundaries are kept or, if necessary, redefined. Boundaries of place include where to meet in order to protect confidentiality on the one hand and to safeguard against any risk of misunderstanding, abuse, exploitation or false accusation on the other. Careful consideration should be given to such issues as when and where to meet, whether others are present in the building, arrangement of furniture and lighting, appropriate body posture, language and dress. It is the minister's responsibility to ensure that furniture and lighting in their own home create a welcoming and friendly atmosphere, without allowing informality to slip into, or be interpreted as, inappropriate intimacy.

3.4 Time boundaries

Boundaries relating to the time spent together are always important. Ministers need to develop skill in establishing a sensitive balance between firmness and flexibility. It is good practice for the minister to suggest how long the meeting might be for and to check whether this is a convenient length of time for the other person. There will be occasions when it is appropriate to extend the time boundary. This should be done by mutual agreement, without losing the sense that there is a boundary. It will then be easier for the minister to bring the meeting to a close if he or she can no longer sustain attentive listening or feels that the person is making inappropriate demands.

Sometimes people who talk non-stop, or raise important issues just as the meeting is due to finish, do so (whether consciously or not) in order to hold their listener and prevent the meeting from ending. If this pattern develops, the minister may need to be very clear from the start as to how much time they have available, warn the person when the time is nearly up and, if necessary, gently but firmly interrupt, perhaps saying, 'We will need to draw to a close in a few minutes . . .' Ending is always primarily the minister's responsibility and sometimes, even when the person is still distressed, it may be advisable to end a meeting and agree to meet again, rather than continue into emotional exhaustion on both sides. Failure to maintain clear time boundaries can result in both parties feeling unsafe and out of control. There is then a risk that, even without being aware of what he or she is doing, the minister will begin to avoid meetings with the other person. Maintaining clear time boundaries is a skill which may take practice to develop but, in the long run, will be beneficial both to the minister and to those for whom they care.

3.5 Dual relationships

When we interact with another person in more than one role we form dual relationships, bringing the possibility of confusion about role and the risk of transgressing boundaries (Gula 1996). Examples would be a parishioner being the minister's GP or car mechanic, or the minister relating to a parishioner as spiritual guide and as a friend, or to the head teacher of a local school as a school governor and as a pastor. Some dual relationships, such as being the patient of a GP who is also a member of the congregation, may be unavoidable in a rural area, but ministers should try to anticipate the pastoral consequences if a professional or commercial relationship with a parishioner becomes problematic and then affects the pastoral relationship. Often dual relationships can be managed without difficulty when things are going well, but they become much more difficult to sustain when problems arise in one role relationship which impact on another role. There is also the risk that the minister's own interests will confuse their ability to judge what is appropriate or ethical behaviour in a pastoral relationship and that, whether consciously or not, they will use it to meet their own personal needs.

Dual relationships are inherent in most forms of ministry and ministers have to develop skills in managing the overlapping roles they hold in relation to members of their congregations. This requires the minister to be self-aware, to focus on keeping the pastoral role as the primary relationship, and to pay careful attention to any potential for role conflict or 'leakage' between the different roles. Parish ministry would be impossible if rigid boundaries about dual relationships were insisted upon. The varied contexts for relating in parish ministry can be extremely challenging to the minister's skills, but can also be a catalyst for healing and integration for both parishioners and ministers. However, the inequality of power in pastoral relationships demands particular sensitivity to boundary issues. Allowing boundaries to become too fluid or to be muddled by dual relationships is a potential hazard which can be damaging for both minister and parishioner. Pastoral ministers (like other professionals, such as doctors and legal advisers) have a professional duty to evaluate their dual relationships carefully and to maintain ethical boundaries (Gula 1996; Syme 2003). Ministers must never exploit a parishioner financially, sexually or emotionally, or in any other way.

3.6 Touch in the pastoral care of adults

The appropriate use of touch is a key aspect of maintaining ethical boundaries in pastoral care. During the 1960s and in the following decades, many ministers and parishioners found a new freedom and appreciation of the power of touch to heal, affirm and show care. In recent years this freedom has been threatened by increasing concern about the incidence of abuse in pastoral relationships.

Touch is now an integral part of worship, and may include the laying-on of hands, anointing with oil, the greeting of the peace, and the foot-washing liturgy of Maundy Thursday. The informality of pastoral ministry can also give a freedom to hug, to kiss and to extend other friendly gestures of touch in a way that would not be open to any other profession. Touch can show care in unique and important ways that communicate much more deeply than words. When people are hurting, afraid, seriously ill or going through bereavement, sensitive touch can offer deep comfort and communicate compassionate understanding. However, people at times of crisis are also extremely vulnerable and require great sensitivity and care. The element of risk lies in the very potential of touch to be a healing, sacramental sign in ministry or to be misused in ways that violate personal boundaries. Touch is integral to the ministry of Jesus, but no minister should assume that because Jesus used touch in a particular way it is right for them to do the same. Each culture forms its own norms about touch. We must be faithful to Christ's mission in ways that fit our own times, always using the language of touch with utmost sensitivity and respect for the personal boundaries of the other person (see pp. 103–4).

The reality of sexual abuse in our culture increases the need for awareness of how easily physical expressions of care and comfort may be misunderstood. It also requires that we have a profound understanding of our own needs and do not mislead ourselves into believing that our touch is for the healing of another, when in reality it is an expression of our own needs or erotic interests. In our culture there is a very strong association of touch with sex so that, whatever the minister's intention, any form of touch has the potential to be received as a personal intimacy with sexual interest, causing confusion in the recipient (Gula 1996). Physical gestures of human caring can easily be confused with romantic, sexual interest, especially if accompanying words are ambiguous.

Men, probably more than women, may now be very self-conscious about their use of touch and may feel unable to discern whether it is appropriate or whether it may be construed as abusive. As a result, some may feel that the only safe option is to avoid all but the most formal physical contact. However, ministers also have to remain sensitive to the reality that, at moments of deep human distress, such as bereavement, a rigid avoidance of physical contact may in itself be damaging. They also need to be self-aware enough to recognize that, at the other extreme, an over-readiness to touch may be feeding the minister's own needs, or be experienced as abusive.

We need to be very aware that touch within pastoral care relationships, even when intended to be affirming and supportive, can easily become touch that makes the receiver feel conflicted, confused or uncomfortable, or touch that is experienced as manipulative, coercive and frightening. In *Ethics in Pastoral Ministry* (1996), Richard Gula suggests that, if we are not to assume that all touch is inappropriate or unethical, we need to develop guidelines to help us differentiate between appropriate, confusing or damaging touch. The following guidance draws on his reflections:

- In relationships of unequal power, it is unusual for the less powerful person to initiate touch. It is therefore essential to be sensitive to any form of asymmetrical power relationship and for the minister, as the more powerful person, always to seek explicit permission before touching. This applies, whether the touch is in the form of a hug, laying-on of hands, a blessing, or involves participation in liturgy such as foot-washing. When touch is offered within liturgy this should be made clear at the time of invitation. Alternative approaches should be made available for those who wish to receive communion or the ministry of healing, but are unable to cope with being touched.

- The other person's freedom to refuse any form of touch must always be respected. We all have the right not to be touched. Touch that we are not free to refuse will always be potentially damaging. There must always be sensitivity to the reality that there may be times when a person cannot cope with any form of touch or physical contact. Some people who have been sexually abused have great difficulty with 'the Peace', which is now an accepted part of many church services and often involves hugging and kissing. Many who have been sexually, physically or emotionally abused do not want to be touched at all, particularly by anyone of the same gender as the perpetrator of their abuse. If there is hesitation or refusal of touch this should always be accepted without question. It may be for a variety of reasons and the person should not be challenged, nor should there be any attempt to interpret or speculate on why they feel this way.

- In relationships of unequal power, such as pastoral care relationships, the perspective and judgement of the less powerful person must have priority. Whether a touch is appropriate, confusing or damaging depends not on the intention of the minister or on how it appears in public, but on how the recipient experiences it. Culture, emotional and psychological state, past experiences with touch (particularly experiences of child or adult sexual abuse), present life situation, relationship with the person touching and the context, will all affect how touch is received.

Ministers who offer touch in pastoral care need to be willing to learn about their own ability to use the language of touch with sensitivity and discernment. For example, a hug can be given in a way that is oppressive, controlling or sexual, or in a way that is gentle and communicates safety and respect. The same may be true of the laying-on of hands or other touch within a liturgical context. It may seem embarrassing to ask a friend, colleague or parishioner whether they feel comfortable with the way we hug or touch, but that may be necessary in order to learn to offer touch in ways that are healing and compassionate. It may also be helpful to create carefully structured training opportunities where different forms of touch, both liturgical and pastoral, can be experienced in a safe context with opportunity for accurate feedback.

Reflection – boundaries in pastoral care

- If someone asks to see you urgently, how do you assess whether to respond immediately or to wait?
- How do you establish and maintain boundaries of time when you arrange a pastoral meeting?
- What relationships are you involved in where you hold more than one role (e.g. parent at local school and pastor to head teacher) and what problems could arise, if there were difficulties in one of these role relationships?
- If you consider it appropriate to offer touch in the context of pastoral care, how do you ensure that you do so sensitively and ethically?

- When leading a service involving touch (for example in blessing at the altar rail), how do you ensure that everyone knows what to expect and can opt out if they prefer?

3.7 Self-disclosure and mutuality

Self-disclosure and mutuality in pastoral relationships also raises important questions about boundaries. It can be appropriate for ministers to share aspects of their own vulnerability with parishioners. However, when ministers disclose information about themselves or share issues which have affected them personally, they need to reflect carefully on their motivation for doing so. Self-disclosure by the minister can sometimes establish a greater degree of equality in a pastoral relationship, but there is also a risk that it will be used, albeit unconsciously, to manipulate a response from the other person. There is a difference between the minister acknowledging difficulties which they have faced in their lives which are now resolved and sharing current issues, such as problems in their marital or family relationships, which may engage the other person's sympathy and lead to over-involvement. A minister cannot assume confidentiality if they share information with someone to whom they have a pastoral care responsibility. If they ask for confidentiality there is a risk of burdening the person with secrets or creating an inappropriate climate of secrecy between them.

Mutuality can arise in minister–parishioner relationships, particularly when the minister is known to be going through a time of personal or family crisis, such as illness or bereavement. Trusted parishioners, such as churchwardens or ministry team members who share responsibility in the parish, may need to be made aware of difficulties in the minister's life, and senior staff and area or rural dean informed so that they can give support. However, parishioners entrusted with such information must understand that whatever is shared with them is confidential, unless the information is officially made public (4.8–10; 5.13–15; 5.17).

If there is a risk that information about personal difficulties will leak out, a clear public statement needs to be made to the parish or benefice, so that rumour and misinformation are minimized. Advice on this should be sought from the archdeacon or bishop, and the diocesan communications officer may also need to be involved. It is natural and appropriate for parishioners to express concern and offer support at such times, but sometimes this can be overwhelming for the minister and his or her family. It may therefore be important to give parishioners guidance on how the minister (and/or the minister's family/close friends) wish to manage the situation, so that they are not continually responding to well-intentioned but emotionally exhausting enquiries, particularly in public situations (4.8–10).

Even when information about personal difficulties is in the public domain, there is a difference between acknowledging that there are difficulties and using pastoral relationships for personal unburdening. Ministers should avoid sharing in ways that may lead to over-involvement and confused boundaries in the future. They need to resist discussing their publicly acknowledged personal difficulties in one-to-one pastoral relationships where their role is to offer care and support. Usually simple thanks for concern expressed and perhaps a brief sentence acknowledging the situation will be enough to satisfy the enquirer.

Ministers always need to reflect carefully upon those relationships where they are aware of a growing sense of mutuality and should be willing to be transparent about acknowledging them to their spouse, spiritual director, colleagues in ministry or ministerial consultant/supervisor. Mutuality can be positive but secrecy or resistance to acknowledging the true depth and mutuality of the relationship to an independent person is often a sign of potential risk.

A regular opportunity to talk through ministerial issues in a confidential setting, whether provided on a peer basis by a priest colleague or by a lay person with relevant skills, is an essential safeguard and support for clergy, faced as they inevitably are by extremely complex issues in pastoral ministry. Ministers who do not have any such regular support are placing themselves at increased risk (4.5; 4.6).

3.8 Over-involvement

Ministers have to be aware of their own needs and vulnerabilities if they are to recognize when psychological and emotional boundaries are in jeopardy, either because of their own unmet needs or the needs or projections of the other person. There is most risk when there is a powerful combination of the two. For example, the minister who is experiencing difficulty in their own personal relationships, is feeling lonely or struggling with feelings of failure in ministry or loss of faith, may be particularly vulnerable to the person who is experiencing similar difficulties and who offers the minister a strong sense of being needed and valued. A vulnerable minister might sense the parishioner's warmth and affection. The minister's own need to feel loved and cared for may then undermine their ability to recognize the abuse of pastoral trust involved, if they respond by seeking to meet those needs through the parishioner.

If ministers become conscious of such responses in themselves or those they are helping, it is essential to seek confidential support and guidance as soon as possible. Many ministers will recognize that there have been times when their own vulnerability could have put them and a parishioner at risk. Ministers who are aware of the kind of situations that may tempt them to become too personally involved, or alternatively to retreat or reject, can face these issues realistically. They are probably more likely to recognize when they need to take particular care and/or seek outside help than the person who assumes that they would never be tempted in this way. Pastoral care demands a high degree of self-awareness and sensitivity to qualities of closeness and distance in relationships. Regular supervision or consultancy can provide a context in which such feelings may be identified in their early stages and appropriate safeguards established. Such confidential support can enable the minister to maintain their capacity to feel for the parishioner's need, while resisting the temptation to use pastoral relationships to meet their own needs. It can also help identify whether the minister's own difficulties are such that they should seek additional help through personal counselling and therapy (4.5; 4.6).

3.9 Warning signs of over-involvement

The following are some of the warning signs of the minister's potential over-involvement and should be attended to:

- becoming preoccupied with thoughts and fantasies about a particular parishioner, dreaming about them or lying awake at night thinking about them
- finding pretexts and excuses for seeing the person or failing to tell spouse or colleagues about meetings with the parishioner
- talking about the minister's own needs and interests and divulging personal information to the parishioner
- exchanging personal or significant gifts and concealing this from others
- taking particular care of appearance when meeting the parishioner
- seeking or allowing unnecessary or lingering physical contact
- tending to avoid a parishioner or experiencing anxiety and embarrassment about meeting them on their own or with others present
- underlying fear of attraction or sense that there is an element of risk in the relationship.

Once again supervision is the best safeguard, enabling the minister to monitor his or her inner world with the support of someone with a more objective view.

3.10 Sexuality

Sexuality is God-given and intrinsic to our humanity. Our sexuality has a powerful influence on all our relationships, whether between men and women or members of the same sex. It draws us out of ourselves and into relationship with others and in this sense sexuality is linked to spirituality. Both are aspects of our yearning for communion and wholeness, ultimately satisfied only by God. Our sexuality should not be a barrier to grace but a means of grace, but because it affects all our relating at a very deep level, it has the possibility of enhancing or damaging the creative and healing potential of our relationships. It is when the influence of our sexuality upon us is unacknowledged, unrecognized, denied or feared that it can seem to take on a power of its own and become potentially damaging to pastoral relationships. Sexual feelings can easily overwhelm and distort rational thought and undermine our ability to discern that it is contrary to God's will to betray committed relationships or to abuse the trust inherent in pastoral relationships.

3.11 Sexuality and intimacy

Our understanding of human sexuality and its expression is still limited but it is usually accepted that, as a result of differences in physiology and socialization, male and female sexuality are experienced differently. Men's sexual energy seems to be more focused on genital expression and women's more diffuse and therefore more capable of sublimation. However, these are broad generalizations and within each gender there is a wide spectrum of attitudes and responses.

We live in a culture in which the sexual dimension of relationships is constantly emphasized, with relatively little attention given to the development of intimacy. In such a climate it is commonly assumed to be impossible to have an intimate relationship without giving it sexual expression. However, in reality, genital sexual expression can be an escape from the costly demands of intimacy, and sexualizing intimate relationships can be a way of staying in control and avoiding the vulnerability of true intimacy (Nelson 1992). It is probably still true that men, more than women, are socialized to respond to intimacy in this way. In consequence, a man may seek to sexualize a relationship with a woman who is offering him pastoral care, interpreting her warmth and compassion as sexual attraction. Or he may interpret a woman's desire to share her spiritual experience at a deep level as indicating sexual interest. In either circumstance, the man may then blame the woman for arousing his sexual feelings, when what the woman actually sought to offer or receive was pastoral support and spiritual communication. Alternatively, anxiety about vulnerability and fears about a latent sexual dimension may make men afraid to develop in-depth pastoral care relationships with either women or men. In contrast, women seem to more readily develop relationships with other women in which there is a depth of intimacy and mutuality without anxiety about the relationship becoming sexualized. Women may model their pastoral care relationships with both women and men on the mutually supportive relationships which they are accustomed to sharing with other women. In consequence they may not be prepared for the possibility that the other person may seek to sexualize the relationship (5.18).

Male and female ministers need to be sufficiently at ease with their own sexuality not to feel threatened when issues of sexuality arise in a pastoral care relationship. If they are secure in their own sexual identity they will be more able to establish and maintain clear and appropriate boundaries in their pastoral care relationships with both women and men.

3.12 Projection and transference

For both women and men in ministry, expressions of compassion and love, including the openness of prayer in a one-to-one relationship, can lead to emotional intensity and inappropriate intimacy and result in unforeseen over-involvement. Sharing deep feelings and personal information creates an atmosphere of intimacy and closeness, in which powerful feelings of love and tenderness may arise and sexual feelings be stirred in the one being helped and/or in the minister. The feelings themselves can seem akin to the experience of 'falling in love' and the person being helped may interpret them in this way.

This projection of positive feelings occurs in a variety of helping relationships and the feelings are not in themselves wrong, but they should be carefully monitored. They can easily distort the minister's judgement and be misused and expressed in ways that are both harmful and abusive. Although it may be appropriate for the minister to acknowledge feelings of friendly warmth and affection, it is potentially dangerous and confusing to explore the depth or intensity of their own feelings, particularly sexual feelings, with the person they are helping. Supervision or ministerial consultation is the context for acknowledging and exploring such issues safely and ethically.

The person in the helping role should be constantly aware that such deep feelings, whether their own or the other person's, may arise from the transference of feelings or projection of unresolved needs from earlier relationships. These intense projections often come into play in helping relationships where there is dependency and depth of interaction. This possibility is a recognized phenomenon in counselling and therapy and counsellors receive training and supervision in how to deal with it ethically. However, clergy minister in a much less structured context and may therefore find themselves facing these complex and challenging issues with minimal preparation or support.

Ministers also need to be extremely cautious about touching the other person, because of the risk that their own needs and sexual feelings will be communicated, even by seemingly 'neutral' touch, and even if this is not what they intended (3.6 and see pp. 103–4). Once again regular ministerial supervision or consultancy is an essential context for exploring such complex issues. Where this is not already established and issues relating to sexuality arise, the minister should seek the help of an experienced ministerial supervisor or trained counsellor, with whom they can talk safely, without putting the pastoral relationship at risk (4.5; 4.6).

Confidential outside support is always strongly recommended if the person being helped expresses intensely positive or negative feelings towards the minister. They may be unconsciously testing the minister in complex or confusing ways, which may originate in early experiences of abuse or deprivation. Unless the minister has some understanding of what is happening and maintains good boundaries, he or she may react to behaviour which feels seductive, manipulative or potentially abusive by reacting angrily or suddenly withdrawing from the relationship without explanation. Alternatively, the minister's sexual feelings may be aroused and he or she may succumb, thus repeating previous patterns of abuse or exploitation. It is essential that the boundaries of the relationship are made clear without rejecting the person. If the person is then unable or unwilling to accept these boundaries, it may become necessary to bring the pastoral relationship to an end, explaining firmly and calmly that the minister is doing so for the protection of both of them. It may also be appropriate to guide the person towards obtaining more clearly structured professional help, such as counselling. It is always the responsibility of the minister to hold a clear, ethical boundary, however much they may feel pressurized or manipulated by the person they are helping (3.3; 3.4).

Reflection – self-disclosure, over-involvement, intimacy, attraction

- What influences your decisions as to whether, when and how to acknowledge personal or family difficulties, or to share aspects of your own personal experience, with a parishioner?
- What issues or difficulties in your personal life or ministry could place you at risk of over-involvement in a pastoral care relationship, and what might be the warning signs?
- What is your experience of intimacy within non-sexual friendships with either women or men?
- How would you safeguard ethical boundaries, if you had strong sexual feelings or feelings of attraction towards someone with whom you had a pastoral care relationship?
- In pastoral care relationships, how would you respond if the other person expressed intensely positive or negative feelings or sexual feelings towards you?

3.13 Sexual abuse of adults by ministers

Any non-consensual sexual contact or sexual contact that occurs when one person takes advantage of another person's vulnerability is sexual abuse. Any sexual encounter in a pastoral relationship is sexual abuse, because of the inherent inequality of power in the relationship and the vulnerable position of the person receiving help (Rutter 1989; Gula 1996). Compliance cannot be taken as meaningful consent, even though the relationship is between adults (CTBI 2002).

Even where there is no actual sexual activity, there may be emotional and psychological abuse, if the person offering pastoral care is using the person they are caring for to satisfy inappropriate emotional and psychological needs. A sexual relationship between two people where one has pastoral responsibility for the other should not be described as 'an affair', but should be clearly identified as an abuse and exploitation of the pastoral relationship. The minister, whether lay or ordained, always carries the responsibility for safeguarding sexual or emotional boundaries, and all ministers, lay or ordained, need to be clear about this. The abuse of power and betrayal of trust involved when sexual or emotional abuse is perpetrated by ministers of the Church is likely to cause immense and irreparable emotional, psychological and spiritual damage to individuals, family relationships and to the church community (CTBI 2002; Chevous 2004).

No one is safe from the possibility of personal and sexual temptation, but tiredness, disappointment in ministry and low self-esteem will make the minister more vulnerable. Nurturing the sexual dimension of a minister's own marriage is important and where there are sexual difficulties in the marriage, or if the minister does not have a sexual partner, the minister needs to recognize that he or she may be at increased risk. However, the power of sexual arousal and fantasy makes it impossible for anyone to be entirely secure. Even a strong faith, a good marriage or a caring life companion, together with adequate theology and conviction, are no ultimate safeguard. Everyone, whether married or single, needs to be aware of the potential risks arising from the intensity, intimacy and lack of firm boundaries that are characteristic of many pastoral encounters.

3.14 Risks and safeguards

Perhaps more than any other carer, clergy are faced with potentially risky contexts for their pastoral work. Ministers with pastoral responsibilities are inevitably placed in situations of vulnerability. They may be visiting vulnerable people in their own homes or meetings may take place in the minister's home with no one else present in the house. Interruption is unlikely and Christian expressions of love and compassion can be misinterpreted. In such circumstances the minister may feel vulnerable and anxious about the possibility of sexual harassment, abuse or false accusation, or some element of physical risk or threat. It is always important to pay attention to such anxieties. Often we know things at an intuitive level which we would find hard to explain rationally. Feeling anxious or afraid will, in itself, bring insecurity to the encounter and increase the level of risk for both parties. Ministers should always try to identify whether their fears are rooted in reality. For the protection of both themselves and the parishioner, they should discuss their anxieties and feelings about the situation with a colleague or consultant who offers appropriate confidentiality. They can then plan sensible, calm action to avoid undue risk.

Where a minister is at all concerned about a prospective meeting, he or she should establish safeguards by, for example:

- alerting a trusted colleague or parishioner;
- ensuring others are in the building or aware of the time and whereabouts of a visit;
- asking someone to be available to ring in or call after an agreed length of time;
- making it clear to the other person that others are aware of the meeting.

Clearly issues of confidentiality must always be considered when setting up safeguards of this kind. However, there may be times when issues of safety take precedence over confidentiality. Sometimes a minister may have to refuse to meet unless there is first agreement that they may inform an appropriately responsible person.

3.15 Children at risk

God was incarnate as a child and for Jesus children were a sign of the kingdom. Children should have a special place in the church community and all ministers have a responsibility to encourage and protect them. Children are always vulnerable and therefore open to being abused in relationships. For many, trust is already in doubt because of the breakdown of relationships between or with their parents or carers. Ordained and lay ministers may be providing pastoral care to children who have already been abused and are therefore especially vulnerable. Our society has become keenly aware of and concerned about the physical, sexual and emotional abuse of children and both professional and voluntary carers need to recognize the need for procedures to safeguard children. It is essential for ministers to recognize that they may have unmet emotional needs and never to use children to satisfy such needs in any way. Ministers must avoid any behaviour that could lead to the misuse or abuse of a child or young person's trust and which could result in a lifetime legacy of spiritual, emotional and psychological damage. Any abuse of children by those in positions of responsibility and trust within the Church does incalculable harm to the children concerned, and undermines the Church and the credibility of the gospel.

All ministers have a responsibility to be aware of current diocesan guidelines for the protection of children and young people and should seek the advice of their diocesan child protection adviser about any allegations or suspicions of child abuse (1.16).

3.16 Touch in the pastoral care of children

Diocesan child protection guidelines give guidance on boundaries with regard to touch and children. In today's climate of anxiety about child protection issues, those involved in the pastoral care of children are particularly in need of training and support. They need to develop their understanding of how to discern between appropriate and necessary touch, and touch which could be misinterpreted or damaging. They should understand the risks involved in working alone with children, including the difficulty of dealing with an emergency and the risk of an accusation against a leader when there is no witness. Touch should always be related to the child's needs and should normally be initiated by the child. Adults must avoid any physical activities that are or may be construed as sexually stimulating to the adult or child.

97

3.17 Adult survivors of child sexual abuse

In recent years the Church of England has implemented measures to protect children from the risk of sexual abuse, but in many churches there is still a lack of understanding of the pastoral needs of adult survivors of child sexual abuse. As a result, survivors can feel unheard and damaged by their experiences of church. *Time for Action* (2002), produced by Churches Together in Britain and Ireland, is a significant resource for increasing awareness of the issues faced by adult survivors. As it is extremely difficult for survivors to speak openly about their experiences, personal accounts, such as Sue Atkinson's *Breaking the Chains of Abuse: A Practical Guide* (2006), are also important in giving insight into the experiences of survivors who are Christians and the often devastating consequences of child sexual abuse.

Sexual abuse occurs in every social group. It is extremely difficult to obtain accurate estimates of levels of sexual abuse, but it is clear that it is common in every stratum of society and usually perpetrated by someone known to the victim. Jeanette Gosney, whose booklet *Surviving Child Sexual Abuse: Supporting Adults in the Church* (2002) offers helpful guidance to enable parishes to give effective support to adult survivors, quotes figures from the Rape Crisis Federation Wales and England 2001, which estimate that 1 in 4 girls and 1 in 9 boys are abused before the age of 18 years. This means that in every congregation, and among ministers and their relatives, there are likely to be an appreciable number of individuals who are survivors of some form of child sexual abuse. Although evidence suggests that more women than men are affected, this may be partly because it can be even more difficult for men to acknowledge that they have been abused in childhood.

Many survivors of sexual abuse find ways of living positively despite their experiences. Others continue to struggle with the effects of the abuse, while some have never told anyone about the abuse, or have repressed all memories of it happening. Most survivors of sexual abuse are likely to experience times when they struggle with the continuing emotional and psychological impact of the abuse upon their lives (CTBI 2002). Some will also be survivors of other forms of physical and emotional abuse.

Children who experience rejection, emotional or physical abuse or are from emotionally distant homes may be more susceptible to the 'grooming' attention of perpetrators, who often target particularly vulnerable children (Gosney 2002). Damaged boundaries and the need for love and affection may also make such children particularly vulnerable to sexual abuse in adult life.

All forms of abuse violate physical and emotional boundaries. A person who has been sexually abused may only be able to protect their personal boundaries by retreating from relationships and not allowing anyone to get near them. Or their confusion about appropriate boundaries may cause them to behave in ways that make them vulnerable to further emotional or sexual abuse. It is therefore especially important that pastoral care relationships offer the security of clear boundaries, even if the person seems to test those boundaries. The very complex interpersonal dynamics which can arise when supporting someone who has been abused, particularly someone who has been sexually abused, mean that the skill, knowledge and defined boundaries offered by a professional therapeutic relationship with someone outside the parish may be advisable (CTBI 2002). However, it is important not to pressurize someone into seeking professional help or into divulging the abuse, because this can be experienced as a repetition of earlier boundary violations. Where counselling or psychotherapy are appropriate, pastoral support can continue to play a valuable part in the healing process.

Survivors who are struggling to find healing from the effects of child sexual abuse may be deeply affected for months, years or even decades, as painful memories surface and difficult feelings are acknowledged or expressed for the first time. The survivor may need a great deal of understanding and support from family and friends. For both the survivor and those close to them, the support of the church community can play a significant part. However, ministers offering pastoral support should have an understanding of the emotional, psychological and spiritual issues that survivors of child sexual abuse face, otherwise they may cause further damage by inappropriate interventions and responses.

The following are some of the issues which can affect survivors of child sexual abuse who, as Christians, want to be able to participate fully in the life and worship of the Church:

- inappropriate teaching around forgiveness with pressure to forgive prematurely
- feelings of shame, inappropriate guilt, pollution and self-hatred reinforced by teaching about sinfulness, sexuality and purity
- difficulty in expressing anger and rage in the climate of 'nice-ness' which often characterizes church life
- language which can trigger experiences of abuse (including words like blood, flesh, body) and language which emphasizes the power and control of God the Father
- difficulty in being in close proximity to other people or sitting and standing with others behind them
- difficulty with the unexpected in worship, such as being asked to talk and share with someone they do not know
- practices in worship which may trigger experiences of abuse (placing of communion bread on the tongue, unexpected or unwelcome touch in the Peace or in healing services, kneeling to receive communion from a minister of the gender of the abuser).

Issues of trust will always be crucial in offering pastoral care to someone who has experienced sexual abuse. Because most sexual abuse is perpetrated by someone already known to the victim, the damage of the abuse is compounded by the betrayal of trust. Pastoral care needs to offer the experience of healing relationships in which there is warmth, love and care without the betrayal of abuse or the pain of rejection. The survivor may need to check constantly and test out relationships which offer affirmation and love, because the rekindling of hope can also bring the fear of further pain and rejection. The survivor may be very afraid of risking dependency and yet also very much in need of relationships in which they may safely be dependent as part of their search for healing. It may take a survivor many years before they can begin to trust that the betrayals of the past will not be repeated. The minister offering pastoral support needs to be realistic about the commitment they are making and sure that it is something they can sustain in a dependable way.

3.18 Survivors of adult sexual abuse

Survivors of any form of sexual abuse in adulthood, including violent sexual assault by stranger, friend, family member or spouse, may experience similar difficulties to those faced by survivors of child sexual abuse. Pastoral care must be offered to them with comparable sensitivity, safety and awareness of the way their personal boundaries have been violated. They may also experience similar difficulties in reconciling their faith, worship and participation in church life with their experience of abuse. It is very hard for anyone to divulge that they have been raped or sexually assaulted, but for men it may be particularly difficult.

Reflection – risks and safeguards

- How conscious are you of the risks of emotional and sexual abuse in helping relationships?
- If you are uneasy about seeing someone when there is no one else in the building or within earshot, how do you safeguard yourself and the other person?
- If you work with children, how do you discern the appropriate way to respond, if they seek or appear to need some form of physical contact from you?
- What could you do to ensure that your church community and worship enable a person who has been sexually abused to feel safe and accepted?

3.19 Litigation and indemnity insurance

We live in a society where increasingly people resort to litigation when professional carers do not live up to expectations of good and ethical practice. There is an element of risk in offering pastoral care, and clergy and other ministers need to be aware that they may at times be vulnerable. Self-awareness and sensible safeguards are essential. The use of touch may be interpreted as abuse or threat. Being alone with a child, woman or man could draw accusations of threat or abuse. Parents' proper concern for the protection of their children could result in unwarranted accusation. A minister's work will be brought to an end by a proven allegation. It may be jeopardized or severely damaged, even by an allegation that eventually proves to be unfounded. In the event of any allegation against them, clergy should contact their archdeacon immediately and may then be advised to consult the diocesan registrar for legal advice.

Clergy (but not non-ordained ministers) may have insurance cover for certain circumstances provided through their diocesan board of finance, but this will not automatically include all clergy in a diocese. Such insurance is important in providing cover for legal costs associated with defending a criminal prosecution and could apply to clergy facing prosecution in connection with alleged abuse. It may include the defence of an insured person's legal rights prior to the issue of legal proceedings when dealing with the police, where it is alleged that the insured person has or may have committed a criminal offence. A summary of the relevant insurance policy cover should be available from the diocesan secretary.

There are also insurance policies available which provide indemnity to parochial clergy for legal liability to pay damages and costs arising from any neglect, error or omission in the provision of pastoral care services. For an additional premium and subject to certain conditions, it may also be possible to extend parish insurance to include similar cover for the provision of professional counselling services. Parishes without such a policy are unlikely to have either pastoral care or professional counselling cover. Clergy, church workers, churchwardens and others should obtain information on insurance for pastoral care or professional counselling either from their diocesan office or from relevant insurance companies. In the event of a potential insurance claim, the insurers must be notified as soon as possible.

THE LANGUAGE OF TOUCH

Touch is a subtle yet powerful language with variable meanings, depending on form, timing and context. It is therefore open to misinterpretation and misuse and must be used with sensitivity and self-awareness. Hunter and Struve (1998) identify categories of touch on a continuum from accidental through to sexual:

- accidental: for example, brushing or bumping against someone, often giving rise to feelings of awkwardness
- task-orientated: for a purpose, such as helping someone out of a chair, or when a nurse takes a pulse or a minister anoints with sacramental oil
- attentional: to gain or hold attention, for example alerting someone to their turn, also includes courtesy touch for greeting, farewell or touch in the Peace
- celebratory/affectional: expressing positive regard, usually reciprocal, may be friendly, helpful, nurturing, caring, encouraging, comforting, joyful
- emotional/expressive: to convey gratitude, reinforce a point, to protect, offer emotional support or convey disapproval
- aggressive: impulsive, disregards boundaries and may cause physical harm
- sensual: for example, soothing caresses or tender embrace (without sexual stimulation) within an intimate relationship, between close relatives or friends
- sexual: communicates overt or implied sexual interest or intention.

Aggressive and sexual forms of touch are unethical and extremely damaging in pastoral care relationships. Sensual touch is easily misinterpreted as sexual and should therefore be avoided or used only in very exceptional circumstances, where the meaning cannot be misunderstood and is open to scrutiny. Accidental touch, although unintentional, implies inappropriate intrusion across personal boundaries and should therefore be acknowledged with an apology, so that it is not misinterpreted. Task-orientated, attentional, celebratory/affectional and emotional/expressive touch may be appropriate, but context (public or private) and timing are crucial. All should be used with utmost sensitivity, caution and transparency. To avoid ambiguity or misinterpretation, explanation should be given and permission sought for all forms of touch, unless there is no possibility of doubt, misinterpretation or offence. The risk is of using (consciously or unconsciously) seemingly appropriate touch to disguise inappropriate meaning, or of appropriate touch being misinterpreted by the recipient.

4

Living Well in Ministry

He said to them, 'Come away to a deserted place all by your-
selves and rest a while.' For many were coming and going, and
they had no leisure even to eat. And they went away in the boat
to a deserted place by themselves.

Mark 6.31–32

4.1 Self-awareness

Every minister has emotional needs and vulnerabilities and will
frequently be exposed to the needs and vulnerabilities of others.
It is therefore essential for the minister to develop self-awareness
about his or her own spiritual, emotional, psychological and
physical well-being. As is clear from the previous chapter, failure
to know oneself adequately can lead to using others to satisfy
unmet needs under the guise of ministering to them. Or it may
eventually result in the breakdown of the minister's mental or
physical health or personal relationships. Personal reflection and
a willingness to receive feedback from others are all important in
developing this essential self-awareness.

4.2 Prayer and sacrament

Prayer and sacrament are fundamental to sustaining good ministerial practice and for ordained ministers the daily office is an
essential spiritual discipline. Many lay ministers also find that
the daily office supports their ministry and holds them securely
within the praying community of the wider Church. Beyond
these essentials, different personalities find different approaches
and rhythms of personal prayer helpful and these will vary at

different stages of life as ministers are led to discover new dimensions to their relationship with God. All pastoral care needs to be rooted in a life of prayer and without this the minister is putting him- or herself at spiritual risk. If ministers are working so hard that they are too tired or too busy to pray, then it is a warning sign that their life in ministry is out of balance.

Priests regularly celebrate the Eucharist, but will also benefit if they are able to receive communion at services where they are not responsible for leading others in worship.

4.3 Spiritual direction

Some form of spiritual direction, spiritual accompaniment or soul care is essential in sustaining all forms of ministry. Vocation in response to God's call to serve others happens in and through the community of the Church, not in isolation. Vocation needs to be supported and renewed through relationships within the Christian community, which deepen faith, spiritual awareness and understanding. All ministers need the discipline of regular opportunities to reflect upon the outworking of their call to ministry, their spiritual journey and life of prayer, with a trusted spiritual director, soul friend or companion. We are not meant to be self-sufficient in our ministry, and sharing with another person can provide the opportunity for new insights, spiritual renewal and inner transformation. A spiritual director needs to be a person, lay or ordained, for whom a deepening relationship with God through prayer is central and whose own inner journey enables them to offer others the hospitality of a safe, confidential and listening space. Dioceses may keep lists of those who are available as spiritual directors and some people undertake training for this role, but usually it is a matter of networking to find the right person.

4.4 Theological reflection

Theological reflection provides the vital link between prayer, Bible reading, theological exploration and what we actually do in our life and ministry. It is disturbingly easy for ministers, even those who regularly spend time in prayer, Bible study and spiritual reading, to fail to make links between these and the reality of their ministerial practice. Theological reflection is the regular discipline of subjecting specific situations and pastoral issues to rigorous appraisal in the light of theological insights, understanding and application. Such reflection can reveal discrepancies between our belief and our practice, particularly if it is carried out in a group or with a peer partner within a context offering safety, support and challenge. Other people can bring the minister new insights, help to liberate from stuck patterns of thought and action and question assumptions about self and beliefs. As with prayer, different approaches to theological reflection may be needed at different stages in our development if we are to be renewed and transformed in our ministerial practice.

4.5 Ministerial consultation and supervision

The demands of pastoral ministry also make it essential for the minister to have somewhere safe to unburden some of their own emotional stress, and to evaluate how the pressures of ministry affect them, as evidenced by their thoughts, reactions, feelings and fantasies. A minister relying entirely on their spouse, life companion or close friend for support in ministry is putting this relationship under excessive strain. While a spouse or friend can be a useful critic, emotional involvement means that their responses are more likely to be subjective and biased towards the minister's point of view. There may also be areas which the minister cannot share with them because of confidentiality, or because to do so would feel threatening to the relationship itself. Ministerial supervision or consultation with a competent person outside the parish can safeguard good practice in ministry and help the minister gain insight into how their own inner life and personal relationships affect their response to the needs of others and vice versa.

The minister needs a willingness to be open to their own inner experience in relation to their work and to be able to explore this with their supervisor or consultant without feeling threatened or becoming defensive. Effective supervision or consultancy should offer a relationship of trust and confidentiality, within which the minister can feel safe enough to explore his or her ministry to individuals or groups, including both negative and positive feelings, attitudes and fantasies, even those which may seem unacceptable or threatening. The primary focus is ensuring good practice and effectiveness in ministry, but personal issues arising from or impacting on the minister's work may also be explored. (However, professional counselling may be needed, if such issues predominate.) It is important that the supervisor has good listening skills and is able to be a confidential and trustworthy companion through times of difficulty and doubt. They also need a good understanding of and empathy for the context and culture of Christian ministry. Having established a relationship of trust, the supervisor should offer appropriate challenge, without undermining the minister's confidence in developing his or her authentic personal style of pastoral ministry.

This form of support could be with a supervisor or consultant from the counselling profession or with an appropriately skilled and experienced spiritual director or minister with enough distance from the pastoral setting to safeguard confidentiality. It could also be in the context of peer supervision with a lay or ordained colleague, but both need to be aware of the risk of collusion and there should be sufficient equality in the relationship to ensure a reciprocal ability to challenge (Chevous 2004). There is, in the Church, great untapped potential for clergy to benefit from ministerial peer support and supervision.

Clergy who have had to work in isolation over many years and are unused to reflecting upon their ministerial practice with others, may find it difficult to see the need for supervision or consultancy. Recently trained clergy, who have come from secular employment where professional supervision is accepted practice, are usually more ready to appreciate the need for this kind of support and sometimes disappointed at the lack of it during their curacy and after. Despite the growing recognition of the need for ministerial supervision or consultancy, it is not as yet a requirement in ministry and is usually left to the inclination and responsibility of the individual minister to arrange. The diocesan Continuing Ministerial Education Officer or Adviser in Pastoral Care and Counselling (or their equivalents) may have information on resources available to clergy. However, as with finding a spiritual director, it is usually a matter of networking among colleagues to find a suitable person.

4.6 Counselling and therapy for ministers

Ministers, like anyone else, may have suffered early trauma in their lives and they are also vulnerable to the impact of major life events, such as illness or bereavement. Ordained ministers also face particular pressures from their public social position, from being constantly in the role of helper, where they are exposed to the pain and distress of other people's lives and from being the subject of other people's often unrealistic expectations. When the pressures of ministry accumulate over a long period of time, or combine with a series of major life events or relationship difficulties, emotional wounds from the past may surface and demand attention.

While family, friends and colleagues may be supportive, the confidentiality, skills, experience and independence of a professional counsellor may be called for. It can be a sign of strength and maturity to take responsibility for psychological, emotional and spiritual well-being by seeking professional therapeutic help and counselling. Along with other forms of support, these can play a part in maintaining and enhancing effective ministry. Ordained ministers who have experienced counselling often find that it enhances their ministry, both through the experience of being listened to at depth and through being able to acknowledge their vulnerability and humanity within a safe and supportive relationship. However, counselling and other forms of psychotherapy are not an easy option. Motivation, a recognition that personal growth and change will be costly, and a willingness to be vulnerable, are all essential if the person is to meet the challenge of working through painful issues. Counselling is unlikely to be effective if someone is 'sent' for counselling by a senior colleague, whom it would be difficult to disregard. Successful referrals are most likely to come via someone whose recommendation is based on first-hand experience of counselling.

In recognition of the personal cost of ministry, most dioceses now have confidential counselling services available for ordained ministers and members of their families, often co-ordinated by a diocesan Adviser in Pastoral Care and Counselling. While the way in which counselling is offered will vary between dioceses, confidentiality over both access to and content of counselling is essential and must be safeguarded if clergy and their relatives are to feel confident about seeking therapy provided through the diocese.

Counselling provided by clinical psychologists or psychotherapists employed by the National Health Service requires referral from a GP or psychiatrist and, in most areas, is a scarce resource for which there may be a long wait. St Luke's Hospital for the Clergy, in London, also provides some access to psychiatric help and therapy for clergy and their families. Some Primary Care Trusts employ surgery-based counsellors, usually offering a limited number of sessions, often with an emphasis on cognitive behavioural approaches. Professional fees charged by counsellors and psychotherapists in private practice vary, but may be un-affordable for clergy reliant on a stipend. Most cities and some large towns have a voluntary counselling agency, often founded by Christians, and offering low-cost counselling by profession-ally trained volunteer counsellors. The British Association for Counselling and Psychotherapy is a useful source of information on local counselling resources.

For some clergy it will be very important to see a counsellor who is a practising Christian and is sympathetic to their under-standing of vocation. However, as with any other profession, the practitioner's Christian faith is not a guarantee of professional competence and counsellors will vary in how they integrate their professional practice and Christian faith. For some their faith provides an essential foundation of prayer and support, but they will only make explicit reference to the Christian faith on the initiative of the person seeking counselling. Others see themselves as offering specifically 'Christian counselling', which may be more directive and strongly influenced by their particular experi-ence of the Christian faith.

In contemporary society it cannot be assumed that a counsellor has any knowledge of the Christian faith or the ethos of Christian ministry, so it may be important to clarify such issues at the beginning of counselling. Whatever the counsellor's faith, for most clergy it will be important that their counsellor is open to the spiritual dimension of experience and sensitive to the often complex interrelationship between spiritual, emotional and psychological difficulties, as well as to the particular pressures upon clergy and their families.

4.7 Ministerial review

Ministerial review by senior staff is not the same as ministerial supervision or consultancy and implies a structure of less frequent but nonetheless extremely important opportunities to reflect upon the pattern and development of ministry. This may take the form of regular pastoral visits to each benefice by bishop or archdeacon, offering the incumbent (and others holding the bishop's licence) an opportunity to review their ministry. Effective review depends on the right balance of support and challenge. Where there is insufficient challenge the review may be blandly affirming, while excessive challenge may undermine confidence. Senior clergy involved in ministry review need to develop the skills required to offer useful, appropriate and well-focused critical feedback within a supportive relationship. If carefully and sensitively prepared for and followed through, ministry review can help to build relationships of trust, enhance confidence and enable clergy to feel that their ministry and its context are fully recognized and appreciated by senior staff.

Beyond such a framework of formal review there are other ways of undertaking a more frequent, informal review of pastoral practice. This could involve churchwardens or other colleagues in ministry, and sections of this book could be used to give focus to such a process.

4.8 Support within parish or benefice

A relationship of mutual trust, openness and confidentiality with churchwardens is crucial in sustaining and supporting the ordained ministers of a benefice, particularly the incumbent. It is important that churchwardens recognize that this is a significant part of their role. The incumbent also needs to be able to let the congregation know about times of particular stress (personal or ministerial), enabling them to share responsibility by offering understanding and support. In some benefices a small group, perhaps involving churchwardens, ministry team leaders or other individuals of the minister's own choice, could be set up to enable the minister to share at a deeper level in an atmosphere of Christian love. However, it is vital to ensure that members of such a group are willing and able to offer secure confidentiality. A contract of confidentiality should be discussed and explicitly agreed when establishing the group. Consideration also needs to be given to how such a support group is perceived by other parishioners not invited to participate in it, who may feel jealous or excluded (3.7; 5.13–15).

4.9 Times of family and personal crisis

Inevitably there will be times of family and personal crisis for those who are in ordained ministry. This may be mental illness or breakdown, a serious or life-threatening physical illness, or severe injury affecting the minister or a close family member. It may be a sudden bereavement or a severe relationship crisis, such as marital breakdown. In the event of such an emergency, ordained ministers should immediately inform and seek help from the area/rural dean, archdeacon and/or bishop, who will want to offer practical and spiritual support. (Curates should contact their training incumbent and/or bishop.)

Clergy, who are so often available to others at times of extreme crisis, can too often find themselves without comparable support when faced with a crisis necessitating their withdrawal from ministry at short notice. At such a time, clergy or their family members may feel both touched and overwhelmed by parishioners' expressions of concern by phone, e-mail or personal visit, but receive little practical help in working out how to be released from their ministerial responsibilities. As a result, clergy, or their spouses, may spend the first few days of sick leave or family crisis trying to arrange emergency cover for services and occasional offices.

The situation is particularly difficult for incumbents working in isolation in rural areas, with responsibility for many churches and with few retired clergy to call upon for help. In consequence, clergy often do not take adequate time off during a crisis, because they fear burdening colleagues whom they know are already overloaded or because they simply cannot face the struggle to find anyone to stand in for them. In the long run recovery is likely to be faster if clergy take proper time off to deal with the emergency and its aftermath, rather than struggling on when they are really not fit to undertake public ministry.

When there is a choice between the needs of the parish and the need to give emergency support to a close member of the family, then the minister's priority should be the family. Irreparable damage can be caused to family relationships when, at a time of family crisis, an excessive burden is placed on the clergy spouse or when family members feel that their parent or spouse has given ministerial responsibilities priority over family needs.

Reflection – support in ministry

- How do you safeguard sufficient time for prayer, reading and reflection on Scripture?
- What fresh approaches to prayer (for example meditation, Ignatian or Celtic prayer, prayer through creative arts etc) could you explore?
- What opportunity do you have for theological reflection with others? Is this sufficient to challenge discrepancies between your beliefs and ministerial practice?
- What opportunity do you have to reflect upon your ministry with someone outside the parish? Does this offer a good balance of support and challenge and protect confidentiality?
- How supported do you feel by churchwardens or others in your parish?
- Whom can you turn to for help and support at times of family or personal crisis?

4.10 Emergency plans for times of crisis

Most of us find it difficult to anticipate the times when we may have to face illness or injury to ourselves or to a family member. We prefer to carry on as if we are indestructible and indispensable. Many clergy ignore minor illnesses (some of which may be a sign of lowered immunity due to tiredness and stress) because it seems too complicated to find cover for services (4.28). However, all clergy should have a plan for dealing with crises and have some back-up arrangements for when they are sick. This is vital for clergy in multi-parish benefices.

Clergy should work out a plan, with those who share responsibility for the parish, that could be put into immediate effect in an emergency. This plan should ensure that neither the ordained minister nor their spouse has to work out from scratch how to arrange cover, when their energy needs to be focused on dealing with the crisis itself. This is even more important where the clergy spouse is also involved in ministry and will also need to be released to deal with the emergency. The plan could be part of a deanery scheme for managing time off for sickness and emergencies. (It could be comparable to the way in which clergy in some deaneries draw up a plan at the beginning of each year covering one another's holiday dates and informing funeral directors of these arrangements.) Archdeacons and area deans need ready access to the information, which could also be very useful for managing an interregnum or sabbatical. Once worked out the plan should be regularly updated, perhaps immediately after annual meetings. Computers and electronic messaging should make it straightforward to administer, and visitations by archdeacon or bishop could be an opportunity for checking that an emergency plan is in place. Resistance to facing our human frailty is the main obstacle to setting up a plan and maintaining its effectiveness. It therefore needs to become an established part of good ministerial practice.

A crisis plan should include the following:

- whom to contact in the parish or benefice when the crisis first arises (churchwarden, associate minister etc.)
- whom to contact beyond the parish (area/rural dean, archdeacon, bishop)

- who will receive phone calls and manage enquiries from funeral directors, wedding couples etc. (with at least two names to allow for absences) until the minister can resume responsibilities
- who will take on responsibility for co-ordinating replacement clergy for services, including weddings and funerals (benefice colleague, area/rural dean, archdeacon, bishop)
- what answering-machine message will be left to maintain contact with family/close friends and re-direct parish callers
- an up-to-date list of people in the benefice or nearby, who may be asked to lead services in an emergency
- where to find wedding registers, keys and other essentials.

Priority should also be given, at both deanery and archdeaconry level, to maintaining lists of ministers (lay and ordained) willing to lead Sunday worship and take weddings and funerals in the event of an emergency.

4.11 Tied housing

Living in a house provided by the diocese inevitably impacts on all who share the home. Tied housing relieves clergy of the immediate financial and practical burdens of home ownership, but also creates anxieties about finding an affordable home if the minister leaves stipendiary ministry or when he or she retires. Although, for many clergy, living in tied housing means they live in a spacious and attractive home beyond anything they could otherwise afford, not all vicarages and rectories are well planned or situated where they or their families would choose to live. The house and garden may be larger than they would want (particularly for a single person in ministry) and expensive to heat or maintain.

4.12 Maintenance and improvements

The diocese has to manage church property in perpetuity and decisions about large-scale maintenance or improvements may not always suit the occupants. Lack of autonomy over what improvements and alterations can be made to the property and delays in dealing with non-urgent repairs or improvements can be very frustrating for clergy and their spouses. It is therefore crucial that diocesan staff responsible for the care of property are sensitive to the reality that the vicarage or rectory is both home and place of work to the clergy person. Arrangements to carry out work need to take this into consideration. Diocesan property departments have a significant and often underestimated role to play in the support of clergy. Their staff need to be appropriately trained to be aware of this responsibility. Clergy, likewise, need to recognize the demands that are sometimes placed on diocesan property departments, particularly when seeking to provide for numerous repairs and improvements, often with competing deadlines to enable new incumbents to take up residence.

4.13 House prices

Rapidly rising house prices mean that those who have given up home ownership to enter into full-time ministry have effectively lost their place in the housing market. This has led to enormous variation in financial circumstances between clergy who own or inherit property and those who do not. At one extreme some clergy come into ministry with their own property, an inherited private income or spouse's earned income, and a pension from a former occupation. At the other extreme are clergy who have no resources beyond their stipend and church pension.

Such factors may not be easy to acknowledge, particularly when clergy are expected to live sacrificially. However, they can have a powerful impact on how secure clergy and their families feel. Anxiety about the future can be particularly acute during training and curacy and at times of frustration or unhappiness in ministry. This is likely to be heightened in a context of declining church attendance and insecurity about job prospects and pensions. In consequence, for some clergy, living in tied housing can contribute to, rather than relieve them of, stress and insecurity. These stresses are likely to seem more manageable if they can be acknowledged and discussed openly.

Many clergy would also benefit from seeking financial advice about planning for retirement at a much earlier stage in their working life, so that they can give careful consideration to their best long-term strategy for pension and housing provision.

4.14 Safety and security

Issues relating to physical safety and security can arise for those living in a vicarage or rectory which has traditionally been regarded as a place to which anyone living in the parish may call for assistance and also one to which those who are homeless or destitute may turn for food or other practical help. Clearly it is very important that individuals who are in distress, or uncertain, do not feel intimidated about calling at the vicarage or rectory. However, there is an element of risk involved in this accessibility, particularly in areas where there are high levels of social alienation or deprivation. Other occupants (spouse, children, friend) left alone in the house may feel or be as much at risk from unknown callers as the minister, particularly if the vicarage or rectory is conspicuously placed next to the church and relatively isolated from other houses. Clergy should always be cautious before inviting someone into the vicarage or rectory if they have any suspicions about them, particularly if they are alone in the house. This is one of the many areas of ministry where clergy are called upon to be 'wise as serpents and innocent as doves' (Matt. 10.16).

The isolation of the house and the public role of the minister may also make the property more vulnerable to burglary or theft and care should be taken not to publicize the incumbent's absence from home. In urban dioceses, with many parishes in urban priority areas, this reality is likely to be recognized, but in predominantly rural dioceses, with less obvious social deprivation or alienation, the need to give priority to safety and security may be less apparent and receive less attention. Clergy ministering in urban priority areas within largely rural dioceses may also feel that their security needs are less readily acknowledged.

All need to feel safe in their own home and garden. Dioceses have a responsibility to ensure that all necessary security measures are in place. Clergy should never feel apologetic about expressing concern for the personal safety of themselves or their family and should discuss any need for additional security measures with churchwardens or archdeacon.

4.15 Difficulties with neighbours

In communities of every kind neighbours can be disruptive and difficult to live alongside and disputes can arise over boundaries or noise. A previous incumbent may have raised expectations by the informal access they allowed to their home or garden or by traditions they established in the local community, such as using their garden for the annual fete. Tensions with neighbours can be exacerbated by comparisons with predecessors or by the tendency of some to project negative feelings onto the Church or those they see as its representatives. Disputes with neighbours are always upsetting, but clergy are in a particularly sensitive position in their local community and this may make resolving difficulties with neighbours much more problematic for them. Outgoing incumbents have a responsibility to explain to parishioners that their successor may have a different policy on access to their home and garden. They should also make their archdeacon or bishop aware of any problems with neighbours which might affect their successor.

4.16 Threatening incidents

When an incident occurs at a vicarage or rectory which results in clergy, or others for whom it is their home, being verbally or physically assaulted or feeling threatened by a caller (whether neighbour, parishioner, stranger or intruder), the victim may experience some degree of post-traumatic stress. A prompt response from diocesan staff is crucial. If the diocese appears to minimize the trauma or to be more concerned with damage to property than risk to persons, then there may be secondary trauma from the experience of feeling unheard and uncared for.

There may be potential role conflict and conflict of interest between the needs of the clergy family and the interests of the diocese, particularly when it is the spouse (or other occupant) who has been the victim of an assault or threat. The clergy person will be distressed on their behalf and yet may also feel in some way responsible, since it is their calling which has led to the situation of living in tied housing. The clergy person may also feel a relatively powerless employee of the diocese, while also holding a leadership role in the local church. Any failure to act promptly on the part of the diocese will add to the sense of role conflict and create potential stress in the clergy person's personal relationships at a time when mutual support is vital.

The first and overriding principle should always be the safety and sense of security of the clergy person and those who share their home. Their voices must be listened to and their sense of violation fully recognized. Although any threatening or violating event will be experienced subjectively, that does not make the experience any less real for the victim. Neighbourhood relations, the risk of inflaming the situation further and the possibility of negative publicity all need to be considered in deciding what action to take. However, the primary considerations must be justice and the physical, emotional and psychological safety and well-being of those for whom the church property is their home. It is their home before it is their place of work and without a home which feels safe for them and their family, the priest may not be able to minister effectively.

4.17 Availability and accessibility

The tradition of providing tied housing for ordained clergy is based on the premise that Church of England clergy live in the locality where they minister, and serve all who live within the parishes for which they are responsible. There continues to be a very strong emphasis on living among or as near as possible to the people served. This emphasis is a key way in which ordained Church of England ministers are different from other professionals involved in community care and support, who are now unlikely to be living in the community where their work is based. The development of multi-parish benefices and the innovation of clergy couples living in the vicarage or rectory, but ministering in two separate benefices, have affected the extent to which clergy are now living in the parishes where they minister. However, ordained local ministers, 'house for duty' appointments and active lay involvement in pastoral care all help to maintain the Anglican emphasis on serving the local community.

Wherever the rectory or vicarage is situated, the majority of ordained ministers are still living 'on the job' and this can add considerably to the pressures of, as well as the opportunities for, ministry. All ministers, but particularly those who live in tied housing, have to learn ways of living positively with the demands this situation places on them.

4.18 Risk from expectations of 24/7 availability

Our model for ministry is drawn from the ministry of Jesus, who came to serve and to give his life to others. Vocation to the ordained ministry is vocation to a life of self-giving, but self-denial should not be confused with self-neglect (Irvine 1997). The prayers of St Ignatius Loyola, 'to give and not to count the cost', and of St Francis of Assisi, 'it is in giving that we receive', are deeply rooted in the Christian psyche, but can lead to clergy having unrealistic and damaging expectations of themselves. In the past the expectation may have been that clergy would be available and on call 24 hours a day, 7 days a week, although in practice their lifestyle was often leisurely compared to that of today's clergy. Widespread car ownership, access to phones, text and e-mail create new problems of 24-hour accessibility and intrusion. Unrealistic expectations of availability, whether the minister's or other people's, can jeopardize the minister's health and relationships and could impair the capacity to respond in a situation of genuine emergency.

4.19 Phone and doorbells

Separate phones for home and ministry (with bells which can be switched off) and an answering machine which identifies the caller and redirects calls during time off can offer protection and safeguard rest and recuperation. There can be an assumption that the phone has to be answered at once, even when it is an interruption to planned work or disrupts meals or a face-to-face conversation. It is essential good practice to ensure that pastoral encounters are not interrupted by the minister's phone. Self-discipline may be needed to resist answering the phone or checking who has called during time off. On days off and during holidays it can be better not to invite the caller to leave a message, as messages can lead to pressure to respond immediately on returning to work. Mobile phones can be useful but disruptive and it may be advisable not to advertise mobile phone numbers widely, unless the phone is used only for work and switched off when not on duty.

Where there are many callers to the vicarage, a separate door-bell, preferably one that can be switched off at certain times, can also protect spouse and other family members from unreasonable or disturbing intrusions.

4.20 Electronic messaging

Electronic messaging enables speedy communication at a time of day that suits the message-sender. However, there are also risks. It is possible to write things that would not be said face to face or over the phone and words written or read in haste can easily be misinterpreted. E-mail can create premature or false intimacy in a relationship or encourage giving vent to negative feelings, which might otherwise be expressed with more restraint. The informality of e-mail and the immediacy of response can also speed up communication and bring the risk of misinterpretation, misunderstanding or overreaction.

The wisdom that, when writing an angry or upset letter, it is usually a good idea to allow time for reflection before posting also applies to e-mail. If the content of the e-mail could be difficult to receive, it is usually a good idea to allow cooling off time and never to press the send button when tired or late in the evening.

Ministers also need to protect themselves from disturbing or distressing e-mails, such as messages of complaint or criticism, which could arrive at their home late in the evening or during days off or holidays. A separate e-mail address for ministry can be helpful and, as with the answering machine, self-restraint may be needed to resist checking e-mails when off duty. On the other hand, the expectation of a rapid response means that it is unhelpful to advertise an e-mail address unless it is checked regularly and responded to promptly.

4.21 Privacy

Ministers and their families need time alone, safe from intrusion. Sufficient privacy is as important for them as it is for parishioners. In smaller and more exposed modern vicarages or curate's houses there may not be adequate facilities for parish meetings without unreasonable disruption to family life. Parishioners and colleagues should not assume that the minister's home and garden are semi-public property to which they have right of access, but may need help to recognize this. Ministers and their families also need to work out strategies for protecting each other from excessive availability and from invasion of their personal space.

4.22 'I know it's your day off but . . . '

Ministers can help to safeguard themselves and their immediate family from unrealistic and exhausting demands by being clear about meal times and other family routines. They can also be firm in communicating that calls outside certain times (e.g. before 8.30 a.m. and after 8.30 p.m., depending on the minister's personal circumstances) or on days off are inappropriate, except in emergencies. Not answering the phone or door at agreed times (such as on a day off) can be very difficult to carry through without feeling guilty, but may be a necessary way to protect privacy and time for rest and relaxation. Some parishioners may seem inconsiderate in calling on trivial matters at inappropriate times, but this may be because a previous incumbent has failed to be clear about what is reasonable, or because the current minister has not made known or been firm about their pattern of availability.

Being open with churchwardens, lay leaders and colleagues about vulnerability, personal limitations, tiredness and feelings of guilt can help give clergy permission to be available and accessible in ways that are more realistic. Lay people may only see the advantages and flexibility that clergy have in working from home and do not always recognize the drawbacks and the difficulty of unwinding when feeling constantly 'on call' even when not on duty. Paradoxically, true availability, which enables the minister to be fully present to those they encounter in their pastoral work, depends on being able to resist the temptation to be constantly busy and to use discernment as to how and when to respond to the demands placed upon them.

4.23 Working patterns in ministry and secular employment

Some clergy find it helpful to see their working day in terms of three sessions and, when possible, to plan to work a two-session day. However, for many this model simply does not fit the varied and unpredictable demands of pastoral ministry. It may be more helpful to consider the difference between the pace and rhythm of ministry and the pace and rhythm of secular employment. Clergy need to be sensitive to the pressures faced by people in secular employment. They may also have long working hours, have to bring work home and attend evening meetings, as well as giving time to church activities. However, in most secular employment the clearer separation between home and work means that, once work is finished, home can more readily be a place to unwind and relax without fear of interruption or demand.

There is a particular risk for those coming into ministry later in life, for whom church has been their only leisure activity and source of friendship outside their secular employment. They may also be used to working at the concentrated pace of secular employment, with a clearer dividing line between working and not working and an established pattern of winding down for the weekend. In addition, the demands of training courses often lead to the neglect of other interests and activities creating habits of overwork, which are then continued in ministry. Training incumbents have a responsibility to ensure that curates (whether stipendiary, non-stipendiary or ordained local ministers) safeguard adequate time off and develop a lifestyle in which ministry, home life and leisure interests are properly balanced. They should not model or demand of a curate unrealistic levels of availability and overwork.

The difficulty for clergy living on the job can be that they never entirely switch off from work while they are home, remaining always at some level on the alert for incoming calls or unable to resist slipping into the study to finish off a piece of work or make a phone call. Ministers who are married need times when they are only available to their spouse and family, and those who are single need time when they are only available to friends of their choice or family. This can be particularly difficult to safeguard, when clergy are often busiest in the evening or at weekends, when their family or friends are free. It is especially hard where the spouse is in full-time employment outside the home and cannot share a midweek day off.

Conversely, clergy can experience the stress of not being able to retain a single-minded focus on their work, particularly when other family members are at home during the day and require or demand their attention. They need to be explicit and clear when asking their family or friends to respect the difficulties inherent in working at home and their need for appropriate time to concentrate on their work without fear of interruption.

4.24 Overworking

Overworking to the point where it may cause mental or physical health problems is encouraged in a society where long working hours are the norm and where women, in particular, often carry extremely demanding multiple roles in family and workplace. It is all too easy for someone to conceal feelings of worthlessness and inadequacy by making a virtue of overwork and to be encouraged in this by the one-day-off-a-week culture of the Church. We all have to find a balance between proper self-care and meeting the demands and responsibilities of work and family life. Of course, there will always be times when our need to keep going to complete a task will outweigh our immediate need for rest. However, if a pattern of overwork and failure to take adequate time off becomes habitual, it may be especially hard for family, friends or colleagues to challenge, because it is 'for God and the Church'.

4.25 The discipline of time off

We tend to think of discipline as involving only work or duty, but the day off, retreat and holidays are also the Church's discipline for safeguarding long-term spiritual, emotional and physical health. Study leave and sabbaticals offer opportunities for deeper spiritual and intellectual refreshment and reflection. They are important in sustaining enthusiasm and energy, particularly given that most clergy will work in parish ministry throughout their ministerial lives. It is the minister's responsibility to ensure that he or she observes these disciplines and the responsibility of churchwardens to support and encourage ministers in taking proper time off. Ministers who neglect their own need for rest and relaxation give an unhealthy example to their parishioners. They may also tend to make excessive demands on lay people with responsibilities in the local church, who may also have demanding lives and need to take proper care of their family relationships and friendships.

Senior staff are usually high achievers who have invested a great deal of themselves and their time and energy in work. If they appear to be invulnerable in the face of personal difficulties and to manage superhuman workloads, while taking little time off, they put their own long-term health and well-being at risk. They also offer an unhealthy and unrealistic model of ministry to parish clergy. Senior staff are also called to discipline in their pattern of work, retreat, days off and holidays.

4.26 Holidays

In planning holidays, ministers need to anticipate how tired they are likely to feel during the first few days of being off work, particularly when they have had to work extra hard to arrange cover for their time away. A two-week break may be insufficient time in which to unwind properly. A three-week break allows time to spend the first week resting, the second gradually recovering energy and the third week motivated to be more energetically involved in holiday activities. For some clergy it works well to have a few days' holiday at home first, rather than setting off after a hectic time of tying up loose ends and arranging cover for services and funerals. This may be particularly important for clergy with younger children, for whom the possibility of resting once they are on holiday is out of the question.

Many people struggle with the transition back to work after a holiday and have difficulty getting up to speed again, because the holiday has only been long enough for them to slow down and recognize the depth of their tiredness. They may then return to work with the unrealistic expectation that, having had a holiday, they should be feeling more energetic and enthusiastic after the break. In contrast, a person who has had long enough to unwind properly and reach the stage of enjoying being active on holiday will be more likely to return to work with renewed energy and enthusiasm.

4.27 Major festivals

The tradition of clergy taking time off after major festivals is recognition of how spiritually, emotionally and physically demanding these periods of ministry are for them. Christmas and Easter celebrations can be especially exhausting for clergy with family responsibilities (whether for the young or the elderly), who are often extremely tired after a major festival, just when their family requires them to be an enthusiastic participant in family life. Strategies, such as having the main family celebration the following day, can be introduced when children are very young, but family traditions are usually deeply rooted and once established are not easily changed.

Reflection – availability and time off

- What expectations do your parishioners, colleagues and family members have about access to your home and its use for meetings?

- If meetings are held in your home, how do you safeguard your family's privacy and space?
- How do parishioners know when you can be contacted and when you are 'off-duty'? Do they respect these boundaries?
- How well do you relax and unwind when at home but 'off-duty'?
- How do you protect your ministerial work from inappropriate interruptions from family and/or friends when you are working at home?
- How often do you work through the day and late into the evening?
- How disciplined are you about having a regular day off and taking proper holidays?
- What model of time off, rest and relaxation do you offer colleagues and parishioners?

4.28 Physical effects of stress

Scientific research has led to a greater understanding of the effects of stress on our bodies. Clergy who are well informed about this will be better able to look after themselves and their families. They will be more likely to avoid the pitfalls of overwork or excessive alcohol or caffeine consumption as ways of dealing with stress and will be more aware of the effect of stress on their parishioners.

A very useful and accessible explanation on the physiology of stress comes from Sarah Horsman. This section draws extensively on her book, *Living with Stress: A Guide for Clergy and Church Leaders* (1989), on her presentation to the Diocesan Advisers in Pastoral Care and Counselling biennial conference (2002) and on private correspondence.

When there is a regular rhythm of work and relaxation and a positive attitude, our bodies can be very resilient. However, the finely balanced self-regulating systems for maintaining body functions, such as blood pressure, blood sugar, salt, water and acidity levels, are pushed beyond capacity by a long-term pattern of relentlessly stressful work and activity. Overbreathing is a normal short-term response when increased oxygen is needed for vigorous exercise and is also part of the fight-or-flight response to stress, but if overbreathing becomes habitual it has negative effects on the body. Symptoms may include feeling dizzy, muscle aches and pains, racing pulse, chest pain, palpitations, headaches, disturbed sleep, anxiety and panic, any of which may themselves become an additional cause of stress.

When we are under stress (whether positive or negative) adrenaline is released into the body and plays a major part in enabling us to respond to challenge (fight or flight) by improving performance. This can happen even when the stress is something positive, such as the excitement of a celebration. However, feelings of distress, defeat or despair also trigger the hormone cortisol, which suppresses the immune system, increasing vulnerability to illness. This is one reason why someone who has been subject to excessive stress and distress over weeks or months is often prone to minor illnesses, particularly when they eventually stop for a holiday. If the stress and distress continue long term then they will be vulnerable to more serious illness.

While our bodies are resilient to hard work when we are in a positive frame of mind, a combination of distress and effort can raise both adrenaline and cortisol to potentially dangerous levels. It is then important either to reduce the intensity of effort and distress or to counterbalance the negative effects with extra time for relaxation and for activities promoting feelings of contentedness and well-being.

- Exercise followed by relaxation reduces adrenaline levels. Some people enjoy relaxing, for example soaking in a hot bath with soothing music. Others dislike having to take time out to relax. However, even if they do not enjoy relaxation, they will benefit.
- Activities which promote a sense of well-being and contentedness help reduce cortisol levels. These could include swimming, walking, dancing, cycling, listening to music, making love, painting, gardening, carpentry, birdwatching, photography, or anything else which is enjoyed.

- At times of stress it is harder to safeguard time for relaxation and restorative activities. It will be much easier if there are already well-established hobbies, enjoyable outside interests, ways of relaxing and habits of regular exercise.

4.29 Recognizing stress

Stress is a reality of life which, at moderate levels, brings challenge and stimulation. However, when stress continues at high levels and over long periods, judgement becomes impaired, reducing sensitivity in distinguishing between one's own perceptions and the other person's experience. Such stress may be caused by events in parish or family life, or arise from unresolved inner conflicts. It is also inherent in the complex role responsibilities of ministers who combine such high-profile tasks as leading public worship (often moving rapidly between occasions of profound distress and those of intense joy and celebration) with the complex emotional demands of pastoral care to individuals.

It is in the nature of the symptoms of stress that the sufferer cannot readily recognize them for what they are. It may be difficult to hear concern expressed by family, friends or colleagues. The minister's spouse, family and close friends are often the first to suffer when proper self-care is being neglected, and their observations should always be listened to with attention. When their expressions of concern are ignored this is, in itself, a warning sign, which may go unrecognized until health and relationships have been irreparably damaged.

Symptoms of stress are not a sign of personal inadequacy but should be attended to. A minister who is under stress, ill or experiencing significant strain in his or her own family, should consider whether he or she can continue to be an effective enough listener and support to parishioners. He or she needs to deal with the stress, usually with the help of other people, who might include senior colleagues, ministerial consultant/supervisor, spiritual director, GP and counsellor. Peer colleagues, churchwardens, ministry team leaders, or some other person in the local church, might also help the minister identify ways of reducing stress and/or increasing support. Senior staff need to be aware, so that they can offer appropriate practical and pastoral support.

4.30 Stress and choice of day off

Ministers will vary greatly in what aspects of ministry they find most stressful. It may be chairing PCC meetings, taking funerals, governorship of a school, doing a school assembly or pastoral care of individuals and families. Ministers who are comparatively new to ministry and lack experience in public speaking, and those who are more introverted, can become especially anxious about leading public worship, particularly where congregations are large and there are high expectations. It is normal to have an increase in adrenaline levels prior to and while leading a service, but if ministers have several services on a Sunday or are under pressure to get to each service on time, they may be unable to wind down and allow adrenaline levels to return to normal between services.

After a sustained period of stress, causing high levels of adrenaline, there is often a period of restlessness or elation, followed by a dip, when the minister feels tired, flat and vulnerable to self-criticism and criticism from others. It may therefore be better for clergy who have several Sunday services and find leading worship or preaching particularly demanding to avoid Monday as their day off and to keep it as far as possible for less stressful work. Others, who don't find Sundays particularly taxing, may identify other days of the week when the pattern of their work is particularly stressful and leaves them feeling extra tired the following day. Saturday is usually unsuitable as a day off because of weddings, church events and preparation for Sunday. For most clergy (including those with school-age children or whose spouse works Monday to Friday), it can be better to have another day off in the week, but to do only essential work on Saturdays, keeping the rest of the day free of duties. Clergy who work in the evenings and have a busy Sunday schedule should resist feeling guilty about having this as time off in addition to their regular day off.

It will be beneficial if, whenever possible, ministers keep the evening before their day off clear, so that they can begin to relax and unwind in preparation for the day off. Whatever the minister's individual experience, it is important that they are not too tired to use their day off for activities which are nourishing for themselves and their families and which will, in the long term, help to sustain them amid the demands of ministry.

4.31 Rest and recuperation

Unrelieved stress eventually leads to some form of emotional, psychological, spiritual or physical breakdown, although the form of breakdown will depend on individual areas of vulnerability. When ministers have been through a period of excessive stress leading to 'burnout' or exhaustion they are likely to need medical advice and support and a period of rest and recuperation. However, it can be extremely difficult for ministers to rest properly at home, particularly if they have reached the point of being unable to unwind. Those who have family responsibilities may be unable to get away for more than a few days, although even that can be helpful in breaking the cycle of overwork and exhaustion. A retreat house, with a regular pattern of daily prayer and somebody available to listen sensitively, may offer the necessary safety and support, particularly if staff or community members are already known to the minister. If the minister is too tired to travel far, or cannot be away from family for long, then this needs to be somewhere local. However, it is sometimes important to get right away to a place where there is less risk of meeting colleagues or parishioners and where the minister can be sure of protection from any risk of 'church talk' or of being asked to minister to others.

The Society of Mary and Martha based at Sheldon in Devon offers specialist resources for people in ordained and/or full-time Christian ministry of any denomination. As well as a varied programme of events and activities, they have developed comfortable and attractive accommodation in which ministers can find privacy to rest and recuperate amid beautiful surroundings. They are also sensitive to the importance of avoiding 'clergy shop talk' and of ensuring that there should be no ministering to other guests. These are essential safeguards for any minister in need of a complete rest from ministry. Members of the community will also offer confidential support or advice if requested and have experience of working with ministers at times of stress, illness or at critical stages in their life or ministry. The Society recently produced a report, *Affirmation and Accountability* (Lee and Horsman 2002), offering practical suggestions for preventing clergy stress, sickness and ill-health retirement. They are particularly aware of the pressures and risks of ministry and are trained in a variety of approaches to health and well-being.

4.32 Alcohol misuse

Alcohol consumption is a potentially harmful activity encouraged in our society as an acceptable means of dealing with stress, distress and overwork. Drinking alcohol is taken for granted as a way of unwinding after a hard day and of enhancing enjoyment, enabling people to relax rather than feel anxious on social occasions (although it also has a depressant effect). Meanwhile those who abstain from drinking alcohol may be regarded as unsociable or assumed to have an alcohol problem. These social attitudes and patterns of behaviour are also present in parts of the Church, including some theological training courses.

Advertising promotes the enjoyable effects of alcohol but not its considerable dangers. Despite the fact that 1 in 25 of the population is dependent on alcohol and UK death rates connected with alcohol misuse are estimated to be close to 33,000 per year (Alcohol Concern 2003), there is widespread ignorance of the damage which excessive drinking causes to physical and mental health and to family relationships. When an individual indicates to a colleague, family member or friend that they fear that their own pattern of drinking is getting out of hand, they should always be listened to and their anxieties taken seriously. The causes of problem drinking are usually complex, including availability of and liking for alcohol, genetic predisposition to become alcohol dependent, the need to numb the pain of a trauma such as childhood abuse, or loneliness and unhappiness in personal relationships or at work. Problem drinking and alcohol misuse do not always take place in public and can remain hidden for years. However, once a person's drinking is very obviously out of control they may be labelled 'alcoholic', with all the negative connotations this has of social inadequacy and chaotic lifestyle.

The stigma for clergy and members of their families can be particularly heavy, making it harder for them to seek or to be offered help in good time. The lack of a clear boundary between home and work mean that, although initially problem drinking may be a private matter, there is always the risk of an unexpected caller or an emergency making it public. All ministers need to recognize when their pattern of drinking is becoming problematic to their personal life, is putting their health at risk (alcohol is poisonous to both liver and brain) and has the potential to damage their ministry.

Access to communion wine and pressure to consume excess consecrated wine raise issues for clergy whose family history and genetic inheritance put them at higher risk of alcohol addiction. Options available for the disposal of excess consecrated wine include sharing it with others and disposal in the earth. Disposal is also an important issue because of the risks inherent in consuming alcohol before driving. The risks are, of course, higher for women because of their smaller body mass.

Parishioners may also find it very hard to divulge that a previous history of alcohol addiction renders them unable to receive the wine at communion. The stigma which alcoholism carries in our society means that such issues need to be managed with great sensitivity and in ways which avoid further stigma or exclusion from full participation in eucharistic worship.

Initial advice on alcohol-related issues and advice on safe levels of alcohol consumption can be sought from a GP or by direct referral to a self-help organization such as Alcoholics Anonymous, to Alcohol Concern (a national organization providing information on alcohol misuse) or to local alcohol advisory services. The British Association for Counselling and Psychotherapy also provides information on individuals and agencies offering help with alcohol-related issues. All agencies will safeguard confidentiality. Motivation is crucial in overcoming problem drinking or alcohol dependency and the person will be required to initiate their own referral. Sometimes other family members need help (perhaps from a counsellor or from a self-help group such as Al-Anon) to prevent them from inadvertently sustaining patterns of problem drinking by 'rescuing' the person from the negative consequences of their problem drinking (see pp. 71–7, Drama and Winner's Triangle).

4.33 Balancing work and leisure

The Gospels witness to the need for a rhythm of rest and withdrawal from the demands of ministry and this wisdom is strongly supported by current medical and psychological knowledge. All ministers need to recognize when they are too weary or stressed to give people sensitive, in-depth attention and to know that they too are entitled to time when they can rest, relax and be cared for in the Body of Christ.

Our bodies have a natural rhythm of activity and rest which allows us to concentrate well for an hour or so before we need to take a break. These natural breaks are important for digestion, maintaining immunity and wound healing, as well as for long-term memory and creative thinking. We also have patterns of high and low energy during the day and need to work with these rather than against them, using our best energy for the most challenging tasks and recognizing times of day when we function less well. Most people's energy peaks in late morning, with low energy by mid afternoon, then an early evening rise in energy is followed by decline as the evening progresses towards bedtime. However, some ministers will much prefer to have meetings first thing in the morning, even over breakfast, but struggle to keep going during late evening meetings, while others are happy with evening meetings but might have difficulty meeting with colleagues to say the daily office early in the morning. As ministers get older, most will manage challenging or frequent evening meetings better and sustain their energy through the week if they take a short rest in the early afternoon.

In modern society we tend to ignore these rhythms and to use stimulants or will power to keep ourselves going. However, if the need for rest is constantly overridden, particularly with reliance on too much caffeine, then adrenaline levels and mental activity increase but performance gradually declines as energy reserves get used up. The eventual build-up of tiredness means that, as soon as work stops, we may be too tired to do anything enjoyable. Beyond that we may get to the point where we cannot relax or unwind, and may also suffer disturbed sleep patterns.

Ministry needs to be seen as a long-term project, a marathon and not a sprint. In the long term, a day off a week is not adequate rest time to maintain good health. Clergy who are habitually working under pressure for perhaps ten hours a day, six days a week, without proper breaks for rest and relaxation, are likely to jeopardize their future health, relationships and effectiveness in ministry. As they grow older, clergy also need to recognize that they will not have the energy to sustain the levels of work possible in their twenties and thirties. All clergy need to be aware of the long-term and often permanent damage to health, which can be caused by many years of unhealthy work patterns. Often it is the most dedicated and able ministers who, as a consequence of their commitment to their vocation, eventually succumb to physical illness, chronic fatigue, anxiety or depression.

Each minister needs to find their own way of working out a balance between work, rest and leisure, taking into account their individual response to stress and their physical and emotional energy levels during the course of a day or a week. Finding this balance involves learning to notice the warning signs of long-term stress and fatigue and at times relearning what it feels like to be in a positive, healthily functioning state. The working lives of clergy, particularly those in full-time ministry and working from home, demand a flexible pattern and rhythm of work. It is inevitable that there are times of working under considerable pressure when ministers may be exposed to a great deal of human distress. Sometimes it is difficult to slow down after a period of excessive pressure, partly because of high levels of adrenaline still in the body, but also because more routine tasks have been neglected, giving rise to feelings of guilt in the minister or frustration in those who feel they have been neglected.

It is very important to monitor working patterns and to recognize that, when ministry has been particularly demanding, steps should be taken to catch up on rest and relaxation. Ministers need to learn the art of working at a gentler pace, having a rest during the day, going for a walk or taking extra time off to recover. Those in full-time ordained ministry also need to think carefully and creatively about strategies to sustain themselves in the longer term. This could mean taking an extra two or three days off every quarter to catch up on missed or interrupted days off or weeks when they have worked excessively long hours. Non-stipendiary clergy and ordained local ministers in full-time secular employment also need to ensure that they have regular time off and do not fill all their leisure time with the demands of ministry. Stipendiary clergy need to respect that those colleagues who minister on an entirely voluntary basis are also at risk of being overloaded.

Prayer, the sacraments, time on retreat, study, reading and time for preparation and reflection can get badly neglected when clergy allow themselves to become too busy. A regular daily pattern of prayer, particularly if it includes right-brain approaches, such as silent prayer, meditation, music, painting or other forms of creative prayer, can help to balance times of intense mental or physical activity through the day. Setting aside the equivalent of a day a month to spend in quiet and retreat and giving priority to adequate preparation time for preaching and leading worship are also essential to sustain ministry. Ministers who also give time and attention to nurturing leisure interests which are not simply an extension of their church life, and who encourage parishioners to do the same, will have greater vitality, creativity and effectiveness in their ministry. Making time for regular exercise will also play a significant part in maintaining physical, mental and emotional well-being.

Parishes do not fall apart when clergy set aside proper time for prayer, study and preparation, nor when they go on holiday, study leave, sabbatical or take sick leave. However, parish life can suffer a great deal when clergy become disillusioned, insensitive to other people's feelings or badly stressed as a result of overwork and neglect of their own spiritual nourishment.

Reflection – patterns of work, rest, relaxation

- What is your pattern of exercise, rest and relaxation? What interests and activities do you enjoy which are separate from ministry?

- Where do you think you are on the Human Function Curve diagram (see page 140 below)? If you are at your limit on effort and performance, or on the downslope, what could you do about this?
- What activities in ministry cause you most stress? What helps you unwind after them?
- What are your best times of day for different kinds of work?
- How disciplined are you about taking extra time off after a very busy or stressful time?
- Where can you go for a quiet day of prayer and reflection, free from ministerial demands?
- If you are in secular employment and minister on a voluntary basis, how do you ensure that you have adequate time off to relax and rest?
- Do you hold space in your diary for the unexpected, or fill all your time?
- How disciplined are you about giving something up before taking on new commitments?

4.34 An empty diary

The demands on clergy vary enormously. In parishes where there are many occasional offices, particularly funerals, and in some multi-parish benefices the pressure of essential work can be excessive. However, there are also clergy who experience the feeling that they are an irrelevance in the lives of most of their parishioners and face the anxiety of an empty diary. In a culture where busyness at work is regarded as a sign of status and importance this can be a very unnerving experience.

It can be a particularly difficult adjustment for a newly ordained person to move from a highly structured secular occupation to the largely unstructured life of parish ministry. Much work in parish ministry is self-generated. Once the initial pressures of the welcome and settling-in period are over, a new curate who has had several exhaustingly busy years of training may find themselves with an empty diary and little prospect of taking on substantial areas of responsibility. Nor are new incumbents necessarily faced with a ready-made work schedule. Not having enough to do can give rise to self-doubt and questioning about the value and purpose of a ministry which has been attained through much hard work and personal sacrifice. It can also be a time of loneliness for someone used to daily contact with colleagues at work. The temptation may be to fill the diary by getting over-involved in some complex pastoral situation or in trying to initiate new projects, without sufficient attention to long-term viability. It can take courage to stay with the emptiness of few external pressures or demands and the depression which can come when there is no busyness to occupy the mind's surface.

However, the space which the early months of a new ministry sometimes offer can be an opportunity to develop habits of prayer, reading and time to reflect, which can be an invaluable spiritual resource for future ministry. Curates and new incumbents may need encouragement to use this opportunity to explore interests which may enrich their ministry and to take time to wait, attend, listen, think and pray. Some of the richest ministries have developed out of a willingness to be a presence in the community, waiting to discern God's guidance, rather than rushing in to fill the space.

4.35 Quietness, solitude and prayer

We live in a society in which being busy is generally taken as evidence of virtue and importance. The temptation for clergy is to collude with this expectation, allowing external demands to set the agenda. This is a particular temptation in any occupation where results are intangible. It takes energy and perspective to decide what is the essential work of pastoral ministry, and courage to refuse requests to become involved in well-intentioned peripheral activities.

Developing the capacity to listen at pastoral depth requires a discipline of time set aside for quietness and solitude, rather than getting caught up in constant busyness. Immersion in prayer,

Scripture and sacrament are also essential if ministry is to be sustained. In a society where, increasingly, everyone is too busy, it takes courage to refuse to compete and to take time to develop a tranquillity of spirit which offers a space of welcoming quiet to others, one where they may be able to discern God's voice more clearly (Peterson 1993). Jesus' ministry took place over a very short period of time and the pastoral demands on him were unrelenting. Despite this he gave priority to taking time to rest, to pray alone and to relax with his companions. On numerous occasions he is described as withdrawing into a deserted or secret place to be with God or taking time to rest. During the storm on Lake Galilee, when Jesus was resting and the disciples protested and demanded his attention, he challenged them for their lack of faith (Mark 4.35–41). His willingness to rest made him available for a life-changing encounter with the woman of Samaria at the well of Jacob (John 4.5–30). A minister who takes time to pray and reflect and who gives proper attention to his or her human need for rest and relaxation will be more to ready to discern and respond to unexpected and potentially life-changing opportunities to minister to others.

Reflection – mapping your support network

(These are suggestions; you can do it your own way.)

1 Take a large sheet of paper (A3 or larger) and coloured crayons/pens.
2 In the middle of the paper draw a symbol or picture of yourself.
3 Around this add pictures, colours, symbols or words to represent all the things and people that support you in ministry (e.g. family, friends, colleagues, parishioners, prayer, hobbies, books, music, paintings, silence, sleep, holidays, retreats etc.).
4 Represent your connection to these supports. Are they near or far away? Is the link strong and steady or weak and intermittent?

5 Then add symbols, words etc. to show those things that stop you from using these resources fully (e.g. fear of criticism, lack of time or money, unavailability of these supports).

- What overall impression does your map create? Do you have the kind of support you want? What support is really positive for you, to the extent that you must nurture and maintain it? Is it enough?
- What support is missing? How could you obtain it or overcome blocks to it?
- Develop a specific action plan to improve your support system. Include any help you need to implement it.

HUMAN FUNCTION CURVE

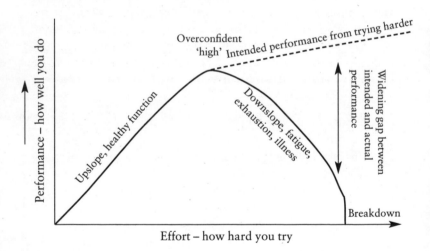

(Diagram adapted from Nixon 1976.)

The Human Function Curve was developed by Dr Peter Nixon (1976). Sarah Horsman (1989) has introduced it as a very useful model for helping clergy to monitor their work. The following summary owes much to them.

- Most of us are taught that if we want to do better we should try harder. When we are on the upslope this is true. We function well, with energy, creative thought, prompt reactions, steady pace and the flexibility to take on extra pressure. When work stops we are able to enjoy rest and relaxation.
- However, at our optimum capacity for effort, working harder will no longer bring improved performance. The overconfident 'high' is the misleading effect of adrenaline.
- If external or internal pressures are relentless and we keep trying harder, we move into the downslope. On the downslope, increased effort does not bring increased performance. Performance and flexibility decline. It becomes hard to rest when work stops and we feel too tired to enjoy time off.
- On the downslope, performance will only improve through working less hard and taking sufficient time to rest and recover. For most people this is counter-intuitive and contrary to what they have learnt.
- Initially the downslope may be gradual, but towards the lower end it gets very steep. The shift into breakdown of health comes suddenly and seemingly without warning.
- The point at which we move from the upslope into the downslope will vary according to our resilience. Resilience will be improved by good self-care, including a pattern of regular exercise, rest and relaxation.

5

The Minister's Personal Relationships

And whoever does not provide for relatives, and especially for family members, has denied the faith and is worse than an unbeliever.

1 Timothy 5.8

I do not call you servants any longer, because the servant does not know what the master is doing; but I have called you friends, because I have made known to you everything that I have heard from my Father.

John 15.15

5.1 Marriage, family and friends

Effective pastoral ministry often depends on the part that spouse, family and friends play in the minister's life. The challenge of balancing the priorities of vocations to ministry, marriage, family and friendship is common to all Christians who take on ministerial responsibilities in the Church. Lay ministers, as well as clergy, may struggle to reconcile the needs of their spouse, family and friends, their work commitments, their call to serve the Church and their own need for rest and leisure time. Like clergy, lay ministers can become overloaded by the ministerial demands on them, and their spouses and families can be neglected. However, the lifetime commitment made at ordination means that those who are called to ordained ministry (whether they are stipendiary or ministering in a voluntary capacity) face these dilemmas in a particular way. The ordained minister's ability to find and sustain a creative balance in their own life and ministry will be a model to others and affect all those with whom they share ministry.

5.2 Ordained ministry, marriage and family

All ordained ministers and their parishioners need to remember that God is involved in both married and ordained vocations and, for many, the vocation to marriage came before a calling to the ordained ministry. However, before the 1960s, few theological colleges recognized the needs of their students' wives and children. Even now, training for ordained ministry, followed immediately by ordination, can put an immense strain on marital and family relationships. Ordained local ministry, part-time stipendiary, non-stipendiary, 'house-for-duty' and dual-role ministerial appointments all raise particular issues in maintaining a balance between potentially conflicting needs and expectations. The Church is also very new in learning to address the issues faced by married women in ministry and by their husbands and children. Senior staff, training courses, training incumbents and parishioners are all having to adapt to unfamiliar situations and may not recognize how deeply ingrained their expectations and assumptions are.

5.3 Expectations on wives and husbands of clergy

In the past it was usually assumed that the wife of a clergyman would regularly attend church, take on responsibilities in the parish and fulfil a public role, simply by virtue of being married to the minister. Such expectations have diminished for women married to ordained men and have never been established for men married to ordained women. However, despite increasing recognition that such assumptions are inappropriate, they are implicit in the desire which some parishes still express, for an incumbent who is married or has a family (who will presumably attend church and not compete for his or her time and attention). Where a previous incumbent's spouse or children have been very involved in parish life it can be difficult for succeeding clergy and family members who do not wish to be similarly involved.

Criticism does not need to be overt to be hurtful to those who are still getting to know the parish and are aware that they are not meeting parishioners' expectations. During the process of seeking and appointing a new incumbent the rural dean and senior staff have an important role in ensuring that parishioners do not have unrealistic and inappropriate expectations of the person appointed, or of their spouse and family.

Where the clergy spouse is actively involved in the parish, this should always be a matter of choice, just as it is for other lay people. Many clergy spouses have their own careers and even where they do not, their active contribution to the life of the parish should not be assumed. Expecting the clergy spouse to act as unpaid secretary, personal assistant or receptionist is inappropriate, unless the spouse feels that this role is something he or she wishes to take on. Assuming that a spouse will do so, without there being a real choice, and disguising this unreasonable expectation in the language of sacrifice or duty, is a form of spiritual abuse (House of Bishops 2001; and see 2.14).

Parishioners may sometimes assume (perhaps from experience with a previous minister) that the spouse knows all about the minister's work. They may want to use the spouse to pass on messages and expect that whatever is shared with the minister is also shared with his or her spouse. Minister and spouse may need to spell out that there is a clear boundary between their relationship and the ministerial role (1.12; 5.6). Spouses can be in a particularly difficult position, if complaints to or about the minister are made through them. The minister's spouse can also feel powerless, hurt and angry when there is harsh or unfair criticism of the minister, but the minister's spouse feels unable to intervene and defend him or her. One way of handling this is to refuse to listen to criticism or complaints and to suggest firmly that anyone with a complaint should speak directly to the minister.

Heavy demands on the minister's time and emotional energy, often working in the evening and at weekends, can also leave the minister's spouse feeling very lonely. He or she may feel isolated for six days a week and understandably resentful at then being expected to be an available companion on the minister's day off. If the spouse is in paid employment outside the home it may be difficult to find any time to relax together.

5.4 Expectations on children of clergy

Some children of clergy very much enjoy being involved in the life of the parish and grow up with a strong faith. Others, perhaps particularly those children and young people whose friendships and education have been disrupted by a parent giving up a secular career and undertaking training in a residential theological college, or those who feel self-conscious or suffer at school through living in the vicarage or rectory, want nothing to do with the church in which their parent ministers. Pressurizing children to attend church will only make the situation worse. If children are to feel valued for themselves, not because they conform to a role imposed on them, then their decision not to attend church must be respected and accepted cheerfully and supportively by parents and parishioners.

Children in clergy families can benefit a great deal from having parents who are more available during the day than parents in secular employment, who may have lengthy and inflexible hours of work outside the home. Clergy do have flexibility and autonomy about a great deal of their work and can plan their time to ensure that they are available at crucial times during the family's day. However, they are constantly having to monitor the balance between their work and family responsibilities and can easily allow ministry to take the best of their relating energy, leaving children feeling resentful and neglected.

5.5 The cost to relationships

The minister's family frequently pays a high price in terms of interruptions and intrusions into family life and in giving the minister freedom to work unsocial hours, often until late in the evening and on Saturdays as well as Sundays. The minister's spouse has to share their partner, and the minister's children their parent, with the affection and attention of many other people, in public and in private. This can only be done if there is mutual trust and understanding between family members and the minister. However, constant meeting with people in emotional need is frequently at the cost of the minister's own emotional resilience and stability. This may be unrecognized, because of a full diary and a wide variety of demands, but if that cost is not attended to it may be at the expense of family relationships. Emotional and psychological exhaustion may take different forms, such as emotional emptiness and loss of contact with feelings, particularly those of enjoyment, love and warmth, inappropriate outbursts of anger and irritability, or retreating from intimacy in family relationships. If marital and family relationships are allowed to deteriorate, there may be a temptation for the minister to seek solace elsewhere, under the guise of ministering to others.

5.6 Couples in ministry

When both husband and wife are involved in public ministry, whether lay or ordained, particular attention needs to be paid to boundaries, trust and vulnerability and to safeguarding quality time and privacy for their relationship. The relationship between husband and wife can be threatened if it has to be the container for all the stresses arising in parish ministry. Nurturing interests and friendships outside the local church will be especially important, otherwise, where both are involved in public ministry, there is a danger that church life will become the only subject of conversation.

Couples who share ministry within a parish also need to be particularly sensitive to the ways in which the depth and strength of their relationship (or difficulties within it) may impact on other members of the ministry team and on the parish. They need to maintain clear boundaries between their ministerial and personal relationships and to be explicit with parishioners and colleagues about how they manage confidentiality.

Where husband and wife are both ordained and minister in separate benefices, extra care will be needed to safeguard boundaries between their respective roles and to ensure that they are not overloaded. Practical arrangements, such as separate phone lines, personal computers and study/office accommodation will be essential and issues of confidentiality can be particularly difficult. Ordained clergy couples are still relatively new in the Church of England and could benefit from linking up with other couples to share experiences and explore different ways of managing the complexities of holding two ordained ministries within one household (1.12; 1.15; 2.25).

5.7 The single person in ministry

At certain periods in its history the Church has valued the vocation to the single life, sometimes to the detriment of marriage. However, nowadays the emphasis on marriage and the family can leave the single person in ministry feeling isolated, even within the church community. Being single may have been chosen as a vocation or it may be the result of a variety of circumstances, including not meeting a suitable life partner, death, separation, divorce or sexual orientation. Whatever the circumstances, a single person can live a richly fulfilled life and singleness may be experienced as a gift, albeit one that may take time to accept with thankfulness. The single person has freedom to choose how they use their time, energy and abilities in both ministry and leisure time, and can enjoy quietness and retreat at home, with a flexibility and choice that is less available to those who are married. However, it is also easy for the single person to neglect his or her own need for rest, relaxation, solitude, spiritual replenishment, fun and friendship.

5.8 Being single and time for relationships

It is important for all clergy to keep up with friends, but for the single person it is particularly crucial to invest time, energy and resources in maintaining good, close friendships and/or relationships with extended family. This may mean higher phone bills and taking extra days off to travel to be with those friends or family. Social life, including holidays away, may take more organizing and it is easy to have no energy for this in the midst of a busy parish life, or to use parish relationships as a substitute for truly mutual friendships (5.15). Unsocial hours (evenings and weekends) mean that it is especially difficult to establish and maintain relationships with those who are not also in ministry or who do not appreciate its demands (5.13–16).

5.9 The single person's responsibilities

A single person living alone has sole responsibility for his or her own emotional, physical, practical and economic well-being. He or she has to attend to all shopping, housework, gardening, car maintenance, arranging holidays, financial management and social life. A single parent has responsibility for children, while other single ministers may be responsible for supporting or caring for parents, a sibling or other relatives and friends in ways that are not immediately visible to others. The accumulated effect of these responsibilities may easily be overlooked by the single person and by others. It is important to be flexible about doing domestic chores within the working day and where necessary to have help with gardening or housework. The single person living on their own also lacks the protection of someone to answer the door or phone at times when they are overtired, unwell or it is their day off. They do not have someone to cancel their appointments when they are ill or in times of crisis. Such times, especially times of bereavement, can bring an intense sense of being alone in the world.

Support networks (friends, spiritual director, ministerial supervisor) are helpful, but may not be available at crucial times, such as after an unexpectedly difficult late-night meeting. When a difficult meeting is anticipated (particularly an evening meeting), it may be possible to arrange for a colleague or friend to be available for an immediate telephone de-briefing.

5.10 The single person's boundaries

If the single person does not have immediate family responsibilities, they may appear to be more available to the life of the parish, but this is not necessarily the case. While they may draw more support from the church fellowship, being both part of the church family but also 'set apart' by their role may bring drawbacks, particularly at times of stress within the congregation. The single person can also feel more vulnerable when dealing with situations in which a parishioner is seeking a closer relationship than the minister wishes or feels it appropriate to offer. It is as essential for the single person to feel free to choose their intimate friends and to establish their own boundaries around their private time and space as it is for the married person. It can be useful to remember that it is not necessary to give an excuse or explanation for refusing an invitation or for choosing to put in only a brief appearance at a function.

5.11 Sexual orientation

We live in a society where we too readily categorize people, labelling them heterosexual or homosexual, as if how we express our sexuality is the defining aspect of our identity. This simplistic labelling denies the mystery and complexity of all human beings and the rich variety of ways in which we relate to members of our own or the opposite sex. Carried over into the life of the Church, it almost inevitably creates stress for those who then find themselves placed in a minority group by virtue of their sexual orientation (2.21).

Research has shown that clergy of homosexual orientation are likely to have higher levels of anxiety, depression and physical manifestations of stress than their heterosexual colleagues. There is a lack of research into stress among lesbian and bisexual clergy, but it seems probable that they too have increased vulnerability. Research also indicates that a major factor in the stress levels of gay clergy is the isolation and tension which they may experience, fearing rejection if they acknowledge their sexual orientation to colleagues or parishioners or if they have a committed relationship with a partner of the same sex. There has been evidence that homosexual clergy ministering in some rural areas feel particularly alone and vulnerable, possibly because of pressure not to divulge their orientation within a closer and sometimes more conservative social network and due to the isolation from others who share their sexual orientation (Fletcher 1990; and see 6.13 below).

Lesbian, gay or bisexual clergy are likely to face particular difficulty in establishing and maintaining adequate social support systems to enable them to manage the demands of pastoral ministry, when there is a climate of controversy. Their support and pastoral care should be a priority to the local, diocesan and national church. Whatever our sexual orientation, the richness of our humanity and the gifts we bring to the Church should not be defined by our sexuality. Clergy of homosexual orientation offer pastoral care to others with as much skill, dedication and faithfulness as do heterosexual clergy. Their contribution to the life and ministry of the Church needs to be recognized, valued and affirmed (2.21).

Reflection – personal relationships and ministry

- How free does your spouse feel to choose whether or not to attend church or to be actively involved in church life? What are your feelings about this?
- How are your children affected by your being ordained? What do you see as the difficulties and benefits for them?
- How do you balance the emotional investment needed to sustain marriage and family relationships, with the emotional demands that pastoral relationships make upon you?
- If you and your spouse are both involved in public ministry (lay or ordained), how do you maintain boundaries between home life and ministry?
- If you are a single person in ministry, how well do parishioners and colleagues respect your privacy? How do you make time and energy to sustain personal and family relationships and responsibilities?
- If you are lesbian or gay, are you able to be open about this with colleagues and parishioners? Do you feel supported and affirmed by them?

5.12 Loneliness in ministry

It can feel like failure and take quite a lot of courage to admit to being lonely, but many clergy are lonely. It is, of course, possible to feel acute loneliness within marriage, although on the whole married people do not have to face what it means to be alone as starkly as the single person. It is important that the minister, whether married or single, does not deal with his or her loneliness by focusing too exclusively on the parish or by using pastoral relationships as a substitute for friendship. Self-knowledge is necessary to discern when a pastoral visit is being made to avoid being alone at home, and this can apply both to the single person or the married person, both of whom can feel isolated through working from home and unsocial hours. Clergy previously used to the companionship of colleagues in secular employment can feel particularly lonely and isolated in ministry. Although both male and female clergy can experience this isolation, female clergy may have more opportunities for finding companionship among other women, who are more likely to be at home in the community during working hours.

5.13 Friendships in the parish

Clergy, like anyone else, need friends with whom they can relax, be themselves and enjoy leisure time. However, it can be difficult for ministers to establish and maintain close and supportive social relationships and personal friendships within the parish community. Until the recent past clergy were often advised to avoid making friendships in the parish and some still hold this view. Others feel that clergy should be able to establish the equality, mutuality and trust of closer social relationships and friendships with some members of their congregations.

It is almost inevitable that being in a leadership position complicates friendship and raises issues, such as projection, jealousy, power and vulnerability (2.3; 2.10; 2.11). This can result in both clergy and lay people experiencing profound pain and disillusionment in their relationships with one another. Such difficulties can be overcome, but this requires self-awareness and maturity from all the individuals concerned and from the congregation as a whole. Ministers could gain from sharing with one another their experiences of both the pitfalls and the possibilities of friendships in the parish. It is also an issue which can be usefully explored in ministerial supervision.

5.14 Levels of relationship

We recognize good marriage relationships as a source of growth and healing, but often underestimate how much we can benefit from the openness, flexibility and challenge of having a variety of friendships. Not all friendships are of the same depth. Individuals in church congregations may relate to one another and to their ministers at any level from the most superficial to the deepest level of encounter.

Andrew Irvine in *Between Two Worlds* (1997) explores these levels of relationship and how they may affect the minister (see pp. 162–4 below). The deeper the relational level the higher the risk if the relationship is damaged or violated. Most of us can dismiss perceived rejection by someone whom we know only superficially. Where we have entrusted another with confidential material about ourselves or the rejection is by an intimate friend or spouse, the long-term impact on health and well-being can be traumatic. Parishioners can be profoundly hurt when the trust they have placed in clergy is broken. It is also important to recognize that ministers and their families can be profoundly damaged if they have trusted a parishioner at a deep level and this trust is somehow betrayed, for example by breaches of confidentiality or harshly worded criticism.

5.15 Emotional, psychological and spiritual demands

The spiritual and personal nature of ministry means that clergy enter into the intimacy of other people's lives, often sharing in their hidden fears and doubts, turmoil and pain. Parishioners trust clergy with some of their deepest experiences, as they face life-threatening illness, tragedy or bereavement or celebrate the joy of marriage, birth and baptism. It is an immense privilege and source of deep satisfaction to be alongside people at such times, but it also makes heavy emotional, psychological and spiritual demands (Irvine 1997). This is often unrecognized by people receiving pastoral ministry and sometimes by ministers. Unless parishioners have themselves experienced being in a helping role or have a natural tendency to be 'listeners' and 'givers' in relationships, they may feel hurt at any suggestion that clergy do not experience the relationship as one of true mutuality.

For many clergy, particularly those in full-time ministry, there can be a discrepancy between the relational level at which they respond to others and the level at which others respond to them. As a result, by the end of the working day the minister may feel drained, with his or her own relationship needs unsatisfied (Irvine 1997). The minister may have insufficient emotional energy to respond at depth to partner or children, while still expecting their spouse to meet all their emotional needs. A single minister may have insufficient emotional energy to sustain close friendships or extended family relationships.

Supportive relationships are a crucial factor in enabling people to cope positively with stress. Lack of supportive social relationships increases the negative impact of stress, thereby reducing immunity to disease and putting physical and mental health and well-being at greater risk (Brown and Harris 1978). If a pattern of insufficient attention to the minister's own need for relating at depth continues indefinitely there will be increasing risk of breakdown or burnout. This may take the form of loss of faith, loss of creativity or compassion, breakdown of physical or mental health, or breakdown in personal relationships. Inappropriate or abusive relationships (involving inappropriate sexual relationships, manipulation or bullying) may be used to satisfy unmet emotional needs.

Paradoxically, it is sometimes when clergy are themselves in deep personal distress and have to acknowledge the extent of their brokenness that they discover the full potential of members of their congregations to offer them pastoral care with a sensitivity and depth which is truly reciprocal (3.7; 4.8).

5.16 Obstacles to friendship in ministry

Most ministers will benefit from some friendships outside their church community, although these can be difficult to establish or sustain because ministers are so often working in the evenings and at weekends, when others have leisure time. In rural areas it may be particularly difficult to establish friendships outside the parish. Newcomers to an area can also feel isolated and cut off from friends in other parts of the country and the opportunities to develop friendships outside the parish may be extremely limited. Friendships need time and energy if they are to be maintained. It is easy for clergy to use up all their 'relating' energy on meeting other people's needs, and to neglect their own need for support and friendship. There can be a time of major adjustment and profound loss for those coming into full-time ordained ministry, for whom their church community was their main source of friendship and support prior to ordination (Burgess 1998). Ordained local ministers may find that ordination affects their friendships, sometimes shifting the balance of mutuality previously taken for granted.

5.17 The parish friendships of clergy spouses

Those married to ordained clergy may be also be affected by the difficulties in establishing friendships which offer true mutuality and reciprocity within a context of trust and confidentiality. They too can feel lonely and deprived of friendships by their spouse's role. They can also be deeply hurt when relationships within the congregation, in which they have placed trust, are undermined or violated in some way.

5.18 Men, women and friendship

Intimacy in friendship means risking self-disclosure, a willingness to be vulnerable and spontaneous and to enjoy the relationship for it's own sake rather than in order to compete or accomplish a task. Male friendships tend to be based on shared activities such as sport or work, often with separate friendships for different activities. Loyalty may be highly valued but when help is requested from friends it tends to be with shared tasks, rather than acknowledging emotional needs or disclosing personal vulnerability. As a result, men tend to have fewer and less intimate same-sex friendships than women and are more likely to rely on their spouse for most of their emotional support (Hahn 1991). For men of heterosexual orientation, an underlying fear of homosexuality and consequent anxiety about physical and emotional closeness with other men can also contribute to a fear of seeking intimacy, affection and validation in same-sex friendships (3.11). Our culture focuses almost exclusively on the sexual behaviour of gay men, but there is also an emotional depth to many nonsexual friendships between gay men, which could be a positive role model for the freedom, intimacy and mutuality possible in same-sex friendships (Nelson 1992).

All these factors are likely to affect relationships between male clergy, and may inhibit the possibility of close, deep and supportive friendships among them. The avoidance or fear of intimacy in relationships with other men may have contributed to the difficulty in establishing all-male clergy chapters as effective places of mutual support. It may also have contributed to the emphasis on avoiding friendships within the parish. Although some deanery chapters work well, it is often difficult to overcome a male reluctance to share at a deeper level. Women who find themselves in predominantly male groups of clergy often find this reluctance a source of frustration. Many male clergy rely on their spouses as their sole source of support, thereby putting a heavy burden on the marriage relationship (5.6).

Women tend to develop greater intimacy in their relationships with other women, sharing and discussing their feelings with more freedom and reciprocity and valuing equality and spontaneity in friendship. Although women clergy do, of course, face loneliness and difficulty in making close friendships, they are more likely to come into ministry with a variety of established close and supportive friendships and to be motivated to continue developing and sustaining friendships with other women in which they can share at depth. However, women also need friendships where they can enjoy shared activities and rest from the emotional demands of pastoral ministry and these may be harder for them to establish. Women's friendship patterns may mean that female clergy are more inclined than male clergy to turn to their friends, including members of their congregations, for emotional support. While friendships in the parish can raise dual relationship issues (3.5), there is much that can be learned from how ordained women develop and sustain friendships within their parishes. It is noticeable that deanery chapter meetings often benefit from the presence of a sufficient number of women ministers to assist in a shift away from male patterns of competitiveness and distance, towards a greater willingness to share at a deeper level.

5.19 Working together in ministry

Colleagues in any work situation frequently spend more quality time with each other than with their spouses. Male and female ministerial colleagues may spend a lot of time alone together, sometimes late into the evenings, perhaps feeling weary and in need of emotional care. Shared commitment to their work may create a strong and deep bond between them and working together may feel more immediately rewarding than some of the everyday demands of family life. This situation has implications which each individual minister should reflect upon. It may be useful to speak openly with both colleagues and spouse about the element of risk at the outset of working together and agree how risk can be reduced, and the integrity of marriage and family commitments safeguarded and protected from threat, whether real or imagined.

5.20 Appropriate behaviour

Men and women working together in public ministry need to be aware of how their ways of relating are perceived by others and to recognize that behaviour which may be appropriate at a personal level may be open to misinterpretation in the 'goldfish bowl' of parish life (Hahn and Nuechterlein 1978). Just as conflict in a working relationship can be destructive of parish relationships, obvious closeness and intimacy between colleagues who share leadership can result in others feeling excluded. It can also give rise to fantasy about the relationship. Awareness of this does not mean colluding with those who would too readily misinterpret behaviour or who are prone to envy or jealousy. A creative working relationship is a gift, but one which requires work and commitment if it is to go on growing. It will be enhanced if it is widened to include others and if there is a quality of transparency about it. We all need privacy if our relationships are to flourish, but an element of secrecy creeping into a colleague relationship is a sign of inappropriate over-involvement.

5.21 Attraction in colleague relationships

Clergy and lay ministers are human and like anyone else they can be attracted to or fall in love with the wrong person. Attraction may be to a person of the opposite or same sex. Sometimes the most deeply committed and sincere Christians are particularly vulnerable, because neither they nor their family, friends or colleagues have ever considered this a possibility. In the past, when behavioural norms were generally those of the Christian Church, it was perhaps easier for the minister's conduct to be single-minded. However, in a society where marriages frequently break down and sexual encounter is openly available, the minister is part of the culture and his or her ideals can be undermined.

There is clearly particular vulnerability where a marriage is already in difficulties or for a single person who longs to find a life-long partner. There will be greater risk if the minister's self-esteem is low, if there is disappointment in ministry, or a crisis of faith. However, the risk is there even where the individual's marriage appears strong or a single person is committed to celibacy. No one should be complacent and assume that it could not happen to them. As more men and women work alongside one another amid the pressures of parish life, the Church will have to face up to the task of learning how to deal responsibly with attraction in working relationships and resist the tendency to scapegoat or blame either women or men when difficulties arise.

5.22 Integrity in relationships

Sexuality and sexual attraction are God-given, but 'our culture's loss of vision of the holy' (Hahn and Nuechterlein 1978) may encourage people to substitute romantic love for the longing for God. If we are already in committed relationships, then we have to find some way of using the positive energy of attraction as the foundation for friendship and creative working relationships. Attraction need not be acted out inappropriately if both parties, whatever their own marital status, are committed to the values and beliefs inherent in marriage. Religious leaders need to live in ways that are authentic to the faithfulness which they preach. People feel betrayed when religious leaders preside over the solemn exchange of marriage vows and yet betray their own. Infidelity is destructive of integrity in ministry and marriage and a minister's infidelity can damage trust within a church community for many years (Hahn and Nuechterlein 1978).

5.23 Attraction, challenge and spiritual growth

In their book *The Male and Female Church Staff*, Hahn and Nuechterlein (1978) suggest that, if a minister is attracted to someone in a working relationship, whether of the opposite or same sex, there are two challenging requirements, whether those involved are married or single:

- To admit the feelings to oneself, even though this is difficult. Only by acknowledging the truth of our feelings to ourselves, can we deal responsibly with them. Denying them to ourselves may lead us to blame or punish the person to whom we are attracted. In the Church, women have suffered from this kind of denial and projection by men, sometimes sustained by a simplistic interpretation of the story of Adam and Eve.

- To recognize and resist the often powerful temptation to act out feelings. Inappropriate sexual behaviour destroys the authenticity of marriage and of ministry. We need to be faithful to our commitments to others and to our calling. However, silence can increase isolation and enhance the intensity of the feelings and associated fantasies. It is therefore of crucial importance that such feelings and desires are discussed with a trustworthy third party not directly involved. This helps to bring realism into the situation.

Holding the tension between these two requirements can be extremely costly, but it is possible, and we need to witness to this in the Church. Falling in love with the wrong person dealt with in this way can, with God's grace, become an occasion for spiritual growth, an authentic experience of death and resurrection. It is important to talk with a counsellor, spiritual director or ministerial supervisor, with the emotional distance to enable calm reflection and sufficiently in touch with their own humanity to accompany someone experiencing inner conflict and turmoil (4.5; 4.6). Such support can help defuse some of the intensity which builds up when two people keep talking together about their feelings for each other. Projection can be a powerful element in 'falling in love'. We may project onto the other person qualities that we value but have not recognized or developed in ourselves. We may also fail to see in them qualities that we dislike in ourselves and may eventually come to dislike in them. If we can own these as aspects of ourselves, then we may learn to see the other person as they really are. Exploring such issues with someone able to be objective can increase self-knowledge and bring realism to the relationship. Feelings also lose some of their seemingly overwhelming power when they are shared with someone less closely involved, who has a realistic perspective on the consequences of behaviour that would be a betrayal of existing relationships (Hahn and Nuechterlein 1978) (3.8–12).

5.24 Single priest and single parishioner

In the past it has been quite common for a single clergyman to find his life partner within the parish where he served as a curate. Until recently no one would have considered this pattern as in any way inappropriate or unethical, and probably, where both parties are single, it would still be accepted as perfectly normal and something to be celebrated. It may also happen with an older ordained person, particularly one who is single through bereavement or divorce. However, even in situations where both parties are single and there is no obvious bar to the relationship, there are important issues which those who are in ordained ministry need to consider.

Before embarking on a personal relationship with a parishioner, it is always essential for the ordained person to examine whether his or her feelings, or those of the parishioner, arise from the inequality and dependency of a helping relationship or whether the relationship has a sound foundation of equality and mutuality. It is all too easy to interpret the intense feelings which can arise in a helping relationship, or the admiration and respect of a parishioner for an ordained person, as 'falling in love'. A relationship based on such projected feelings may rapidly founder once the individuals involved begin to see each other as they really are (3.12).

Lack of privacy in the parish context means that it may be very difficult for two people to gain a realistic experience of each other and to explore the future potential of their relationship without it becoming public. Once the relationship is known in the parish it may also be extremely difficult for either party to withdraw from it. There is then a risk of feeling trapped into making an unsuitable permanent commitment. The ordained person needs to be aware of the consequences for both if the relationship comes to an end, particularly if this is not by mutual agreement. He or she may find it hard to continue ministering in the parish and his or her ministry may be undermined. Alternatively, the parishioner, who may have deeper roots in the worshipping community than the ordained person, may find it hard to continue as part of that community. These risks may be somewhat diminished for a curate who will move after three or four years. They may be much greater for an older person, especially someone who has become single through divorce or bereavement and has little recent experience of exploring new relationships.

It is hard to give calm consideration to these potential difficulties amid the intensity and excitement of 'falling in love', but it would be advisable for a single ordained minister to reflect upon them and seek independent and confidential advice before becoming deeply involved in a close relationship with someone in their parish. Sometimes there may be sufficient trust to take a churchwarden, parishioner or colleague into their confidence, but the objectivity and confidentiality offered by a ministerial consultant may be more appropriate (4.5).

Reflection – working closely with colleagues

- How does your spouse feel about the time and energy you give to relationships with ministerial colleagues?
- If you have close working relationships with ministerial colleagues and spend a lot of time with them, how do you protect and sustain your prior and steadfast commitment to your spouse?
- What effect would it have on family, parishioners, colleagues and friends, if you or another minister became involved in an inappropriate relationship with a parishioner or colleague?
- If you are a single person in ordained ministry and became involved in a close personal relationship with a local ministerial colleague or parishioner, what difficulties could arise for you, the other person, your ministry and the parish? What issues could arise if the relationship subsequently broke down?

5.25 Jesus and friendship

The Gospels show Jesus being friends with a wide variety of men and women, allowing himself to be vulnerable and experiencing both the joy and pain which friendship brings. In John's Gospel a close circle of friends around Jesus provides the context for his ministry. Jesus also offers friendship as an image of our relationship with God, and the Church as a place where we can transcend our differences and share friendship with one another. Jesus took the risk of offering intimate friendship to his disciples, both women and men, revealing himself to them and experiencing the intense pain of misunderstanding, betrayal and abandonment by those whom he had trusted to be his friends. We see that Jesus' relationships with his disciples included both the companionship of shared activities and the intimacy of self-revelation (Hahn 1991). His relationships involved a variation in depth, intimacy and mutuality, sometimes resulting in the difficulties of envy and competition between disciples. The Acts of the Apostles and the Epistles also show how, despite the difficulties which sometimes arose, Paul developed relationships of deep friendship among those with whom and to whom he ministered.

Where lay people place heavy role expectations on clergy or clergy invite these, it will be difficult for them to establish truly reciprocal friendships with each other. However, as churches become places where ministry is shared among a community of equals, rather than being confined to the role of one professional person, then the mutuality of friendship may become more possible. As women and men share together in a varied spectrum of ordained and lay ministries, then their different experiences and understandings of friendship can also enrich and strengthen ministry.

LEVELS OF RELATIONSHIP

The following levels of relationship have been adapted from those identified by Andrew Irvine in *Between Two Worlds* (1997, pp. 91–3):

Level 1: neighbourhood contacts

Relatively superficial contacts in the neighbourhood are important in giving a sense of belonging within a local community. Such contacts might simply involve mutual recognition and acknowledgement at the bus stop or in the local shop, or the encounter may gradually develop into a slightly deeper level of interaction, with exchange of news about family, holidays etc. While clergy may feel it is part of their calling to develop friendly contacts with neighbours, rural areas and suburban housing estates are often empty of people during the day and there may be few opportunities for this kind of casual encounter.

Level 2: work relationships

For many people, work relationships offer a significant source of human companionship, particularly where they are of long standing and involve a sense of shared purpose. Good colleague relationships can offer immense support and satisfaction. Conversely, difficult colleague relationships can cause considerable pain and unhappiness. In secular work relationships, colleagues often get to know quite a lot about one another's personal concerns and patterns of behaviour, and considerable trust and companionship may develop. Clergy often lack such day-to-day contact with working colleagues. During the daytime, working from home can feel very isolated, particularly for those who have been used to working alongside colleagues. Men, for whom it is traditionally more unusual to be at home during the day, may feel this particularly acutely. Women are still more likely to be at home during the day, whether through part-time work, responsibilities as carers, or due to longer life expectancy.

Level 3: social relationships

Most people choose to develop some social relationships with individuals, couples or groups whom they identify as having common interests or characteristics, such as shared social or educational background. They choose to give personal and social time to creating a relaxed atmosphere in which such relationships can mature and trust can develop. It is easier to do this where there is already common ground. Clergy who move to a parish where the social or geographical background of parishioners is very different from their own are likely to have more difficulty in developing and sustaining social relationships in which they can be themselves.

Level 4: depth relationships

A much deeper level of relationship develops when trust and confidentiality enable the sharing of more intimate personal information and experiences. At this level people can relax, let go of the demands of their official position and acknowledge the inner depths of heart and mind with an increasing degree of transparency. For most people, this level of trust and sharing will only happen with a very few others. It may be reciprocal, in deep friendship or close family relationship, or it may be one-way, as with a minister and parishioner or counsellor and client. Clergy are likely to have a number of relationships in which they offer this level of safety and depth to others, but where they do not share in a reciprocal way.

Level 5: intimate encounters

This is the deepest level of interaction. Although it may be in the context of a sexual relationship, deep intimacy is also possible without any sexual encounter. Such relating involves a deepening spiritual and emotional interaction; it may be with a life partner, but could also be with a relative, spiritual guide or intimate friend. In ministry such a spiritual encounter, founded on trust, transcends differences in gender, generation, status, class, colour or education. It may arise when the minister is accompanying someone experiencing intense grief, pain or joy or engaged in a journey of deep spiritual exploration. It can be one of the most profoundly enriching experiences of ministry with a sense of being together on 'holy ground'. However, in pastoral care it is still held within a context of responding to another's needs rather than a relationship of mutuality.

Reflection – mapping your relationships

(These are suggestions; you can do it your own way.)

1 Use a big sheet of paper (A3 or larger) and coloured pens/crayons.
2 Draw a symbol or shape in the middle of the paper to

represent yourself, then add symbols and shapes to represent ongoing relationships (Levels 1–5), whether in the parish, benefice, diocese or beyond, and name them. (You may want to choose a colour for each level.)

3 Place the shapes or symbols on the paper to show how near or far they are from you. Connect the shapes or symbols with lines or marks to show how frequent and reciprocal the relationships are (e.g. a feint or dotted line to show not much contact, arrows in both directions to show reciprocal contact).

4 Use colours, symbols or words to show the depth of any relationships which offer you support, affirmation or a sense of belonging. Identify any relationships which you feel have the potential to be a source of greater mutuality and support.

- How varied and frequent are your neighbourhood contacts?
- How satisfying are your relationships with colleagues?
- How easy is it for you to establish social relationships with friends living nearby, who share a similar education or social background?
- Do you have relationships in which you can enjoy the companionship of shared activities which are unrelated to church?
- How available are such relationships to you?
- What depth relationships or intimate encounter relationships do you have where the other person shares with you but you do not reciprocate?
- What truly reciprocal depth or intimate encounter relationships do you have? How strong are these in terms or frequency and means of contact (face to face, phone, e-mail, letter) or length of time spent together?
- What in-depth or intimate encounter relationships do you have in which you can share deeply, without having to give emotionally in return?

- When you look at your map, how do you feel about the variety, depth and mutuality of your relationships? What would you like to change about your map? With whom could you share your map and work out a strategy for such change?

6

Transition, Loss and Bereavement
in Ministry

*Blessed be the God and Father of our Lord Jesus Christ, the
Father of mercies and God of all consolation, who consoles us
in all our affliction, so that we may be able to console those
who are in any affliction with the consolation with which we
ourselves are consoled by God.*

2 Corinthians 1.3–4

6.1 Patterns of transition and loss in the minister's life

Supporting individuals and families through times of loss and
transition is a significant aspect of pastoral ministry. Ministers
also face times of loss and transition in their own lives; nego-
tiating these while supporting others can place heavy demands on
emotional and spiritual resources. Ministers, particularly those
who are ordained, need to be aware of their own personal history
of loss and transition and to recognize how this may affect their
ability to offer pastoral care to others.

Early life experience has a significant impact on how we
respond to transition and loss in adulthood and also on how we
are able to support others. Ministers who have had secure
attachments to their parents or other primary carers and have
been well supported through periods of transition and loss in
early life are likely to be more resilient in managing transition and
loss in adulthood (Leick and Davidsen-Nielsen 1991).

Transitions bringing both loss and gain are a normal part
of human life. They will include developments such as wean-
ing, starting school, adolescence or old age, all of which are

unavoidable aspects of growing up and growing older. Other changes, such as marriage, birth of children, changing occupation, children leaving home or retirement, are not experienced by everyone who lives a full life span. Even when change is both chosen and welcomed, the loss of a familiar pattern of life and relationships on which we have relied for our sense of identity and security can be very disturbing. Routines and relationships take time to replace and the intervening time of transition may feel chaotic, disorientating and exhausting. If feelings of grief and loss are suppressed, a minister may be unable to re-invest their energy in establishing themselves in their new pattern of life. Their ability to empathize with parishioners going through comparable periods of loss and transition may also be impaired.

Difficult past experiences of loss, whether in early life or adulthood, can make it harder to minister effectively to others who are bereaved. However, the crucial issue is whether the minister has resolved their own grief experiences sufficiently and gained insight into how these may influence their capacity to support other people. A minister who has never experienced a close bereavement, and has only a theoretical understanding of grief or a theology insufficiently grounded in the reality of human experience, may underestimate the arduous task faced by a grieving person. Such a minister may be dismayed to discover how powerless and vulnerable he or she feels and how faith is tested when experiencing a major bereavement for the first time. However, a minister who has worked through their own grief, perhaps with the help of a counsellor, may develop deeper theological insights and a much greater depth of empathic understanding for others (4.6).

6.2 Simultaneous or consecutive loss and transition

It can be particularly difficult for an individual or family to work through their grief if they undergo several simultaneous or consecutive experiences of loss and transition. There may be insufficient time to grieve the first loss before grieving is interrupted by a subsequent loss; or a major bereavement may happen during a difficult period of transition, following a move of home and job. Working through grief is very demanding and resources for grieving may be depleted by multiple losses. The need to keep functioning in order to look after other family members or to sustain ministry may block or delay grieving, until a subsequent event or a period of stress brings it to the surface again.

6.3 Transition and loss in pre-ordination training and curacy

Those who train for ordained ministry in mid-life, and members of their families, often experience several years of transition and loss during the process of pre-ordination training, curacy and moving into first incumbency. The impact on spouse and children of leaving extended family, well-established friends, a familiar and much loved home, schools and work can be enormous and long-lasting, particularly when there may be insecurity about the future throughout the years of theological training and curacy. It takes most people at least two or three years to become settled in a new home and ministry. During training and curacy there is usually not enough time to settle between moves before the next is imminent. This can have a particularly damaging effect on children who are going through the transition of adolescence or preparing to leave home. The disruption will be exacerbated if there are also close family bereavements such as the loss of parents or grandparents. After ordination, major transitions continue as spouse or family adjust to becoming a 'clergy spouse' or 'clergy family' and to the ordained minister working from home. For family, these transitions may be both unchosen and unwelcome.

Meanwhile the new minister may have been so occupied with the demands of theological training and getting established in their new ministry, that they have had little time or energy to attend to their own loss during these periods of transition. The sense of grief at what has been left behind may only catch up with them after ordination. Although many individuals, couples and families come through the training period strengthened and with their relationships and their faith deepened, there are also casualties, with long-term damage to individuals and to marital and family relationships. If training incumbents, senior staff, directors of ordinands and parishioners do not recognize the impact of these experiences on newly ordained curates and their families they may add to the difficulties. Ministers and their families are much more likely to negotiate transition and loss successfully if their feelings of grief can be recognized and acknowledged rather than being suppressed.

6.4 Subsequent transitions in ministry

Even for those well established in ministry, moving home and parish can be an enormous upheaval for all involved. Clergy families often become deeply established in a rich network of relationships in the local church and surrounding community, including schools and employment. While moving in secular life is also difficult, it usually offers more choice for family members, both in terms of where they live and their church community. Clergy families have to take the house and local community that comes with the job, whether or not it is a house and area where they would otherwise choose to live. They may also feel that they have to take the church that comes with the minister's job, even if it is not where they would have chosen to worship. Spouse and children grieving for their home, work, school and previous church may not be ready to build new relationships until they have had time to grieve for all that has been left behind. Meanwhile the ordained minister is required to be enthusiastic in investing energy in building relationships in the new parish.

6.5 Transition to chaplaincy or sector posts

Moves to sector posts or chaplaincies are usually planned for and sometimes long awaited. Often it is a positive choice to move out of parish ministry, perhaps bringing the opportunity to buy a home for the first time. Such posts may also offer the freedom to seek a worshipping community where the minister may contribute without carrying the burden of full responsibility and where the minister's spouse may find a spiritual home. However, even when chosen and prepared for, the experience may be quite disorientating and involve a sense of loss rather than gain, especially if there is difficulty in finding a suitable church in which to settle.

6.6 Transition to senior posts

Ordained ministers and members of their families may find the experience of moving to a senior diocesan post, such as archdeacon, suffragan bishop or senior member of cathedral staff, a difficult and lonely transition involving losses as well as gains. As senior appointments are not applied for, such a transition cannot be planned for. Timing may be difficult for spouse and children and may involve a move to an unfamiliar part of the country that would not have been chosen by either the minister or their spouse. The minister may feel that they have to respond to God's call, but may deeply regret leaving aspects of their previous ministry which gave them profound satisfaction and enjoyment. A clergy spouse may have to sacrifice their own career for the move and, if they were also very involved in the life of the parish, may feel bereft of a deep sense of belonging in their local church. Bishops and archdeacons often work very long hours, involving travel and a heavy burden of evening and weekend engagements, making it difficult to maintain a regular day off. Their spouse may feel lonely and children may be understandably resentful. The minister's spouse may also feel uncomfortable about the role expectations which still cling to those married to senior staff and which can be hard to resist. It can be particularly difficult for both the ordained minister and their family to recognize and work through their difficult feelings of loss about a senior appointment at a time when they are expected to rejoice.

Reflection – loss and transition in the minister's life

- How might your experiences of loss and transition in childhood affect your response to loss and transition as an adult?

- Are there periods in your adult life when you have experienced simultaneous or consecutive losses? What support did you have at those times?
- How do your own experiences of loss and transition influence your pastoral ministry?
- How have you and members of your family been affected by the transitions and losses involved in your training for ministry and subsequent moves of home, parish or sphere of ministry?
- How well prepared were you for these transitions? How do you feel about them now?

6.7 Pastoral care of bereaved people

Funerals and bereavement care usually play a central part in parish ministry and can be among the most emotionally demanding and rewarding aspects of pastoral ministry. Funerals and being with the bereaved offer vital opportunities to care for people, many of whom would otherwise have no contact with the Church. These areas of ministry enable encounter at a depth often not possible in preparing for weddings and infant baptisms. In the immediate aftermath of the death of a close relative or friend, people are often emotionally open and vulnerable in a way that creates great potential for healing and growth, or for damage and hurt.

6.8 Funerals: containing and expressing grief

The funeral, preparing for it and subsequent bereavement care can play a crucial part in enabling close relatives and friends of the dead person to begin the intensely demanding journey through grief. A funeral liturgy carried out with dignity and sensitivity to their needs will help to sustain the bereaved person through this time of bewildering transition. Failures in this regard can cause permanent pastoral damage.

In addition to their spiritual role, the minister at a funeral service has a challenging emotional and psychological task. This is to ensure that the service offers safe containment for some of the most intense and painful feelings human beings are capable of experiencing, while at the same time enabling those present to feel that the funeral is a natural and appropriate occasion to acknowledge and express such feelings.

The task of containing and enabling expression of feelings is all the more difficult because, in our culture, those present may be ill at ease in a church context, unfamiliar with and afraid of death and uncomfortable with intense emotion and its expression. Achieving a positive balance between containment and expression of feelings will depend, in part at least, on how far the minister has been able to find this balance within him- or herself. A minister who is afraid of intense emotions may unconsciously block those attending the funeral from acknowledging or expressing them in the way that they need to.

6.9 Emotional cost of bereavement care

The funeral is a crucial part of the bereavement process. Between the death and the funeral the bereaved person may have experienced the numbness and disorientation that often follow death. The funeral may be the occasion on which they begin to take in the full reality of the death, and experience for the first time the intense pain of their loss.

At a funeral ministers are often exposed to intensely painful emotions, whether or not the mourners express their feelings openly. If the mourners are very self-controlled, ministers may not recognize the power of the feelings to which they have been exposed at an unconscious level. They may therefore not recognize their need for recovery time after the funeral and may absorb and continue to 'carry' feelings of grief, anger and pain which belong to the mourners and not to themselves. Moving rapidly into a different aspect of ministry, such as celebrating a marriage or chairing a meeting, may mean the minister continues to carry these 'absorbed' emotions for a prolonged period. They may later unconsciously project such feelings onto members of their own family or feel inexplicably tired or emotionally drained for days or even weeks after the event.

The greater the sensitivity of the minister and the greater their support to and involvement with the bereaved, the more vulnerable they are likely to be to this unconscious process. Their vulnerability to absorbing other people's feelings will also be increased if they are themselves carrying unresolved experiences of grief or loss, or if the death is one which threatens them in some way, such as the death of a child of similar age to their own. Vulnerability will also be increased if, as happens in some parishes, the minister is taking four or five funerals a week with little respite, particularly in the winter months.

The impact of exposure to such intense emotions is now widely recognized by psychotherapists and counsellors, hence the requirement for them to have professional supervision to maintain emotional health and professional effectiveness. Ministers may be unaware of the potential effect on them of taking frequent or particularly difficult funerals without adequate opportunity to unburden their own feelings. Some form of ministerial supervision or support (4.5) is an important way of ensuring ministers do not get overburdened by the demands of taking funerals and supporting bereaved people. Without such support there is a risk that they will become emotionally and spiritually drained, with the possibility of depression or deteriorating personal relationships. Alternatively, ministers may protect themselves by becoming remote and under-involved, distancing themselves from the pain of those to whom they minister. In consequence some who have had to cope with relatively little support in the past may be critical of suggestions that more support is needed.

6.10 Funerals after death in tragic circumstances

Supporting relatives and taking funerals will be particularly demanding if the death happened in tragic circumstances, such as a road traffic crash, murder, suicide or accident, or if it occurred during a major disaster affecting an entire community. The demands will be increased if there is media involvement. In such circumstances the minister may experience some of the symptoms of post-traumatic stress (irritability, forgetfulness, flashbacks, nightmares, exhaustion, emotional numbing etc.). The minister may also be particularly affected if the death was of a child or young person, or of someone close to their own age or the age of a close family member or friend.

6.11 Taking funerals of close relatives, friends and parishioners

Bereavement is one of the most demanding areas in which ministers have to work with overlapping boundaries between the personal and ministerial aspects of their lives (3.5). In taking the funeral of a member of their own congregation, clergy may themselves be grieving. There may be additional aspects to the minister's experience of loss if the dead person was also in a key church role such as churchwarden or treasurer, especially in a small and ageing or declining congregation where the person may be particularly hard to replace. Similarly, clergy taking the funeral of a non-church-going member of the community may themselves be personally affected, particularly when living in the same or a nearby village community. In all these circumstances clergy will be dealing with their own grief, as well as supporting parishioners and others who are grieving. They may be uncertain as to whether (and if so how) they should share their own feelings in an appropriate way with parishioners. If they do not have time or a safe place to grieve, their own grief may be put on hold and may subsequently affect them in both their ministry and personal relationships.

It has often been the practice for clergy to take the funeral of a family member or close friend. For some this is one of the privileges of ministry, but it is likely to be emotionally extremely demanding. It must inevitably involve the minister distancing her- or himself from the immediacy of grief and being 'in role' and may therefore interfere with them experiencing their grief fully. Clergy should think carefully about whether or not they would want to and would feel able to take the funeral of someone close to them, to avoid making the decision when they may be in some degree of shock in the immediate aftermath of the death.

Reflection – taking funerals

- What do you find most rewarding and most difficult about taking funerals?
- How do you feel and respond when mourners become visibly distressed at a funeral?
- How are you affected when taking a funeral that reminds you of similar or potential losses in your own family?
- How have you been affected by taking funerals in traumatic circumstances such as road crash, suicide or murder and what support has been available to you on these occasions?
- How appropriate do you feel it would be for you to take the funeral of a close relative or close friend?
- If you take the funeral of a parishioner or other local person whom you knew well, how do you deal with your own feelings of loss?

6.12 Recently bereaved clergy

In the immediate aftermath of death it is normal to be in a state of shock, which may take the form of emotional numbness or elation and euphoria. In addition to the pressures of their public role, bereaved clergy, who will eventually move away from the parish, may have difficult decisions to make about place of burial (6.16; 6.24). In such circumstances it is difficult for the minister to assess accurately his or her ability to function effectively. The loss of bearings and diminished self-esteem that can accompany bereavement may make the minister especially anxious to hold onto the security and protection of their ministerial role. Those professionally involved in helping others through bereavement can have unrealistic expectations of their own capacity to cope with grief. A theoretical knowledge of the process of grieving is not necessarily a help when a minister is faced with the over-whelming experience of personal bereavement. Grieving may be particularly complex and difficult if the death happened in traumatic circumstances, such as an accident, suicide or after a long and debilitating illness. The minister may be determined to continue taking funerals at a time when the level of self-control and self-protection which this requires may lead to some denial of their own need to grieve. For clergy there can be the particular danger of using the language of thanksgiving and celebration to deny the reality of their own grief.

6.13 Seeking support in bereavement

Many people in ministry find it harder to seek or receive help than to give it and have to learn to seek support for themselves. One of the new skills a bereaved person may have to learn, at a time when they are particularly vulnerable, is how to ask for emotional and practical help (see pp. 192–3). This may be made harder if colleagues and parishioners feel inhibited about intruding into private grief or afraid to suggest that the minister may not be well enough to carry on ministering and leading worship. However, it can be a gift to both parishioners and colleagues when they are allowed to offer the minister emotional, practical and spiritual support. Jesus not only responded with great compassion to those who were grieving but was also unafraid to weep publicly (John 11.31–37). Ministers need to be aware that if, during their own times of bereavement, they model stoicism and invulnerability, then parishioners may find it harder to turn to them for help and support in their own grief (3.7; 4.8).

There is, from a mental health perspective, a strong case for anyone who has experienced a very close bereavement (e.g. husband, wife, child, parent, other close relative or life companion) being relieved of the burden of arranging and taking funerals and visiting the bereaved for an agreed period. The climate in parish, deanery and diocese should be one in which such a break is seen as professionally responsible, not a sign of inadequacy or inability to cope. Gay or lesbian clergy who lose their life partner may have particular difficulty in finding the support they need in bereavement especially if they did not feel able to be open about their relationship, whether to their family, parish or diocese (5.11).

At a practical level, help with planning an extended period away from work, assistance in taking funerals, sharing responsibility for bereavement support with lay people, seeking help from clergy colleagues who have experienced close bereavement while in office, or the specialist help of a counsellor, are all possibilities. Churchwardens and readers, the area dean, archdeacon or bishop are all potential sources of support and advice (4.9; 4.10).

6.14 Practical and emotional adjustments in bereavement

After the death of a person with whom the ordained minister shared their life, the minister is likely to face stresses not experienced by those who work away from home. The minister will now have to cope single-handedly with all the usual demands of running a household and may have relied on the deceased person for active support in ministry, or for help with taking phone messages, answering the door or offering hospitality. He or she will also lack the social support, companionship and 'escape' from grief, which a workplace outside the home can offer. It may be very difficult to plan time off, with the temptation to keep working to avoid loneliness.

There is likely to be repeated contact with other bereaved people, as part of everyday work, at a time when grief is still acute. Agencies such as CRUSE, offering help to bereaved people, usually do not accept for training as bereavement counsellors anyone who has experienced a significant bereavement in the previous two years. Yet ministers have no respite from responding to the needs of their bereaved parishioners, despite their own grief.

Practical and emotional care of children may be very difficult. Different family members grieve differently; younger children and adolescents may regress or react by acting out their feelings in ways which, to an adult, are not easily recognized as an expression of grief and may be particularly hard to manage in the 'goldfish bowl' of parish life.

For a widow or widower, remarriage is rarely wise until the tasks of grieving have been completed (Worden 1991; Leick and Davidsen-Nielsen 1991; and see pp. 192–3 below). When marriage after bereavement takes place prematurely, as an escape from the pain of grief and an unrealistic attempt at recovering or replacing the dead partner, it can become a source of deep unhappiness for all involved. The risk is that over time the new spouse will sense that they are not known or truly loved for the person they are or they will fail (or feel that they are failing) to live up to the hopes and expectations of them.

6.15 Death of an ordained person in stipendiary or house-for-duty ministry

There are particular emotional and practical difficulties for spouse, children or life companion, when a clergyman or clergywoman dies and they were occupying diocesan property. Specialists in support to bereaved people recommend that a bereaved marital partner should not take major decisions, such as moving house, within less than a year of the partner's death. Yet this is usually not possible for the bereaved partner or other life companion of clergy and she or he may lose home, established social contacts, way of life and church community within a short space of time. The necessity of moving may raise difficult issues about place of burial if the bereaved person will eventually have to leave the parish. Diocesan staff will be as sympathetic and sensitive as possible in such circumstances, but it is important that all clergy and their partners discuss this issue and consider what their choices might be at each stage of their family life and ministry.

6.16 Death of a child in a clergy family

In modern western society it is against all our expectations that a child will die before his or her parents and this will always be one of the most traumatic and potentially isolating bereavements. It is one from which there is, in a very real sense, no recovery. Grief will continue and be felt especially at each birthday and as milestones such as leaving school, graduation or marriage and parenthood are reached by contemporaries of the dead child. The death of a child is a parent's worst nightmare and, in the immediate aftermath of death, other parents may avoid contact because of the subconscious fear that the death of a contemporary of their own children can elicit. The death of a child many years before, or of an adult child not known to parishioners and colleagues, can also bring feelings of isolation.

The decision about where to bury their child is particularly crucial for stipendiary, non-stipendiary and house-for-duty clergy, when the expectation is that they will eventually move and keep some distance from their former parish. Decisions about place of burial are extremely difficult to take in a state of shock and numbness following the death of a child. Parents facing such a traumatic situation may benefit from consulting with a counsellor or with senior staff who have had experience of the longer-term issues involved in such decisions.

The death of a child inevitably places great stress on a marriage as each partner struggles to grieve in his or her own individual way and to work through the anger and guilt which such an event can arouse. Among Christians, particularly clergy families, there is sometimes a pressure to deny such feelings. Other children in the family are likely to be profoundly affected and may behave in ways which add to family stress and tension.

Stillbirth and neonatal death are also forms of bereavement which are now relatively rare in our society, but have a profound impact on parents and other members of the family. Miscarriage can also cause intense grief, and it may be particularly difficult for parents to cope with baptisms and children's work in the aftermath of such bereavements.

6.17 Childless clergy couples

Involuntary childlessness can be understood as a form of bereavement, of lost hopes and expectations for the future, and may involve profound grief and distress. Such feelings may become particularly acute around the time of menopause and may be experienced by both married and single clergy. Sharing about children's progress, achievements and problems is often a significant way of making contact with parishioners, but for a childless minister (and/or their spouse) it can also be a continual reminder of loss. Childless clergy (and/or their spouse) may find in ministry an outlet for their parental feelings, but this can be at great personal cost. The sense of loss will continue as friends', parishioners' and colleagues' children grow up, and can be particularly acute as contemporaries and parishioners begin to have grandchildren. It may also be felt intensely when other couples plan to retire near to their settled adult children, when health begins to fail or in widow/widowerhood.

A parent who, with the death, physical or mental illness or injury of a child, has lost the possibility of grandparenthood may also experience grief akin to the bereavement of childlessness.

6.18 Divorce in a clergy family

Clergy may be particularly vulnerable to feelings of failure if they themselves have to face their own marriage ending in separation or divorce, or if their children face marriage breakdown.

The Christian ideal of lifelong marriage is to be cherished, but we need to be aware of the acute and complex grief experience of those whose marriages are in difficulty or have failed, particularly when they are from among the clergy. Clergy can face particular distress because of their exposed position in the community and because of fear that marriage failure may have a damaging effect on their future ministry. There may also be fear of adverse media interest, although this is very unlikely to arise unless infidelity is involved. Although it would be unrealistic to deny that divorced clergy can sometimes have more difficulty finding a parish in the future, in practice senior staff and parishioners usually respond with compassion and do all they can to offer help and support. In addition to the bereavement of marital breakdown, divorced clergy face similar practical difficulties to those experienced by clergy bereaved through the death of their partner. They too have to make a considerable adjustment to single status and may feel socially isolated and excluded from the world of couples.

Marriage failure rate rises with second and subsequent marriages and clergy are not immune to this trend. The responsibility for failure of a marriage is almost always (though not invariably) shared and it is, therefore, important to work through and understand each partner's contribution to marital failure before embarking on a second marriage. The greatest safeguard to a second marriage is to have faced these issues, to have worked at understanding the underlying causes of the failure, and at healing the damage caused by the marriage relationship itself or its breakdown.

6.19 Severe damage to property of clergy

Clergy and members of their families may be affected by events and experiences involving loss or damage to property. This might include damage by fire or flood or the violation of burglary or theft. Our homes and personal belongings are important in giving us a sense of identity and security. We know that ultimately we can only rely upon God for this, but it is natural and human that our homes matter to us, giving us a place in which we can relax and express our personalities and in which our belongings reflect our personalities and give a sense of continuity through life. When home or personal effects are damaged, destroyed or violated, the trauma can be longlasting. In particular, items such as photographs or objects with sentimental value can never be replaced and will need to be grieved for. Clergy, and of course their parishioners, will also be deeply affected if the church where they minister is damaged or destroyed.

6.20 Disabling or life-threatening illness or personal injury in clergy families

Clergy and members of their families may be affected directly or indirectly by disabling or life-threatening illness or physical injury. Injury might be caused by traumatic events such as physical assault, including mugging or rape, road crash or tragic accident. Disability may be the result of these events or an illness such as chronic fatigue syndrome, stroke, Parkinson's disease, dementia, heart attack, cancer, diabetes or serious mental illness. There may be severe physical or sensory impairment or brain damage. There will be loss and grief whether such events or experiences affect the minister or a person close to them. If the minister is directly affected by disability then they may face early retirement and their spouse or other close companion (e.g. parent, sibling or friend) may become their carer. If they continue in ministry they may become very dependent on their spouse or a parishioner to enable them to continue to work. If it is the minister's spouse or other close companion who becomes physically or mentally ill or disabled, then the minister may become the carer, as well as meeting the demands of ministry. If it is a son, daughter or other close relative the minister and their spouse may be involved in long-term physical, emotional and financial support, in addition to all the demands of ministerial life.

Such experiences may bring many secondary losses, including loss of control, trust, confidence, hopes for the future, self-esteem, faith, security etc. The emotional and psychological response will be akin to grief but may not be recognized as bereavement. It will be a major task to identify and grieve for all the dimensions of what has been lost and to adjust to the new pattern of life and expectations. It can be especially hard to grieve when the relationship with a spouse or other life companion continues but is radically altered by disability. Other people may fail to perceive the enormity of the loss or may be unable to bear the pain of empathizing deeply with the minister's suffering. Ministers who experience these complex, intangible losses may find it hard to make space for their ongoing grief amid all the demands of ministering to others. Continuing support from senior and peer colleagues, friends and parishioners will be critical in such situations.

Reflection – experiencing bereavement in ministry

- If you have experienced the death of a close family member or close friend while in ministry, whom did you turn to for practical help, particularly with taking funerals? Were you able to take sufficient time off before returning to ministry?
- How would you manage your family responsibilities and ministry if your spouse or other life companion died?

- What provision have you made for your spouse or other life companion in the event of your death before retirement age?
- If you have experienced miscarriage, stillbirth, the death of a child, or involuntary childlessness, how has the experience affected your ministry?
- If you have been through a marriage breakdown, how did parishioners, colleagues and senior staff respond? How has the experience affected your ministry?
- If you have been affected by disabling or life-threatening illness or personal injury to yourself or a member of your family, how did parishioners, colleagues and senior staff respond? What effect has the experience had on your ministry?

6.21 Leaving a parish

Clergy and their families usually have to face, several times, the process of leaving a parish. It is an aspect of ministry which can have a profound effect on clergy, their families, their future ministry and the welfare of the parish left behind. Clergy may have very mixed feelings when they leave a parish. They may feel sadness at separating from people to whom they have grown close, excited anticipation of the new and fear of the unknown. Saying goodbye means facing the reality, both positive and negative, of parish relationships and accepting that they will either end or change. Parishioners may have similarly mixed feelings of loss, hope and anxiety.

In *Running through the Thistles* (1978), Roy Oswald explores how reflecting upon habitual approaches to social leave-taking (such as slipping away unnoticed or endlessly prolonging good-byes) can throw a surprisingly accurate light on characteristic patterns in other more crucial contexts, such as leaving a parish:

- clergy may rush through the time between resigning and leaving, to avoid their own and other people's difficult emotions, with the risk that their suppressed emotions will surface in the new parish and affect ministry there

- clergy may be so open and receptive to everyone else's feelings, while suppressing their own that they end up exhausted and depressed; they are likely to enter their new ministry lacking in energy and motivation

- clergy should aim to listen to other people's feelings, while still remaining in touch with and appropriately open to their own experience; a willingness to share the difficult feelings involved in parting can lead to greater emotional freedom and less fear of entering into new relationships.

6.22 The effect of loss on parishes

Many parishes are already suffering from multiple losses, through people dying, moving away, choosing to join another congregation or simply letting their church attendance or involvement lapse. Often, when people leave a church, this happens without proper attention to the process of making an ending. They simply disappear and nobody knows what happened or why they left. A diminishing and ageing congregation and the loss of an incumbent resident in the community also make a congregation more vulnerable to further loss.

Failure to deal effectively with the process of leaving, by denying what is happening and refusing to share feelings, can leave parishioners doubting whether clergy really cared about them. They may feel abandoned or betrayed and wonder, without having the opportunity to check this out, whether they are the cause of the minister leaving. When a minister leaves and a congregation does not have sufficient opportunity to work through their feelings, their unresolved loss and pain may be carried into their relationships with their new incumbent (Oswald 1978). The effect of unresolved feelings will be exacerbated if their resident vicar or rector is unlikely to be replaced, or the boundaries of the multi-parish benefice they belong to are likely to be altered before the next appointment is made.

When approached with vulnerability and openness, leaving can be an opportunity for growth for all concerned. Leaving a parish is bound to be difficult when clergy have worked closely with parishioners over many years and have shared deeply in painful or joyful aspects of their lives. It will be even more complex where there has been unresolved conflict, disappointment or frustration. In such circumstances it may be helpful to ask a colleague from outside the parish to act as 'consultant', to help prepare for leaving and to reflect upon each step of the process (see p. 193).

If the ending of an ordained person's ministry in a parish is dealt with fully, with acknowledgement and expression of the complex feelings that are stirred up by the impending separation, then both minister and parishioners will have more energy available to face the future. While many factors may influence the length of the interregnum, it is usually important for parishioners to experience their loss through sharing responsibility for the well-being and smooth running of the parish in the absence of an incumbent. Parishioners will be more ready to begin their relationship with the new incumbent if there has been adequate time to let go of the previous one and if they have carried some of the ministerial burdens which normally fall upon the incumbent. An interregnum can also be an opportunity for a parish to gain confidence in themselves and to discover their own gifts in ministry.

6.23 Support for clergy family members

Spouse, children or others affected by the move may also need the opportunity to express their feelings about leaving and might value having someone outside the family to discuss this with, without feeling disloyal. The feelings of loss and powerlessness experienced by family members can be profound and may seriously affect future relationships within the family.

6.24 Contact with former parishioners

The Church of England's *Guidelines for the Professional Conduct of the Clergy* (2003) advise:

> On resignation or retirement clergy should . . . sever all professional relationships with those formerly under their pastoral cure. Any exception to this guidance should be formally negotiated with the bishop . . . clergy should only minister in a former church, parish or institution if invited by the clergy with pastoral oversight or with their permission.

However, in parish life a professional relationship is not always clearly defined. Clergy may feel that there are a number of parishioners with whom the nature of the relationship is such that to sever it completely would be damaging for all concerned. This is likely to be true of relationships where a degree of mutuality and a quality of friendship has developed over many years, or where there has been a depth of involvement due to particularly tragic circumstances in the life of the parishioner. Other family members may also have friendships with parishioners which they wish to continue. Such possibilities will, of course, be increased in proportion to the minister's length of service in the benefice.

Clergy can find it particularly hard to make clear decisions about future contact because they leave a parish post not knowing who will succeed them, how long the interregnum will last and sometimes whether the benefice will be split or incorporated into another benefice. They are also not expected to have contact with their successor and are not involved in any kind of pastoral handover. It can be very difficult for a pastorally sensitive minister to leave a vulnerable parishioner, knowing that there may be little continuity of care for them. In such circumstances, and in the heightened emotional intensity of departure, it is easy to get drawn into making commitments which could undermine the pastoral ministry of a successor or which cannot be sustained once the departing minister becomes involved in a new appointment.

The nature of any continuing contact should therefore be clearly defined. For example, the former incumbent may need to make it clear that, for a period of years, they will not visit former parishioners at their homes in the parish, allowing the new incumbent to become properly established.

It can also undermine a new incumbent's ministry if their predecessor returns to take weddings, baptisms or funerals which would otherwise be an opportunity for deepening pastoral relationships. A departing minister should therefore state explicitly that, without exception for friends or prominent members of the church, they will not return to take occasional offices. It is much easier to make such a policy clear to parishioners before the situation arises than to have to refuse a request at a time of bereavement or family rejoicing. If exceptional circumstances do occur during an interregnum, it will then be up to the area dean in consultation with senior staff to consider whether it may be pastorally appropriate to invite the former incumbent to return, and then to discuss with him or her whether they feel able to respond to this invitation. Particular care needs to be exercised when the former incumbent moves to a parish within the same locality.

6.25 Early retirement of clergy

The number of clergy taking early retirement due to ill health has increased in recent years. Sometimes, where the minister is still relatively young, there remains the possibility that they will eventually be well enough to resume ministry. In others, age or prognosis means that a return to full-time ministry will not be possible. For most clergy who have to retire early on health grounds, this is an extremely difficult and painful decision and a major bereavement. There is usually disappointment, sadness, anxiety about health and finance and a sense of failure at having to relinquish prematurely a vocation to full-time ordained ministry. Colleagues (senior and peer) in ministry need to be aware of how difficult this situation is and to offer continuing support if at all possible. Otherwise, feeling forgotten by former colleagues can compound the sense of grief and worthlessness that some experience in these circumstances. Some clergy who have taken early retirement may still be well enough to act as a spiritual director, to offer advice and support to those in ministry, or to preach and preside at the Eucharist on occasions. If this is what they wish and are able to do, they should seek permission to officiate from their diocesan bishop. Even where they choose or are forced to give up all forms of active ministry they may, in their vulnerability and weakness, have a particularly powerful ministry of prayer and witness.

6.26 Retirement from ministry

In our society age is one of the primary ways in which we categorize people. However, 'old age' cannot be accurately defined in chronological terms, because individuals grow, mature and age at different rates. Although 'old person', 'elderly' and 'pensioner' are habitually used to describe anyone over sixty, this does not make a lot of sense when active life may continue for another thirty years. Age is not an accurate guide to health, intellectual ability or a willingness to be open to new possibilities.

Prior to the introduction of the state retirement age, many clergy continued in parish ministry until advanced old age, whether through dedication to their calling or financial necessity. Most clergy who are in a financial position to do so, retire at 65 and many are very glad to give up the responsibilities of a parish at this age. Although some clergy do make a positive choice to stay on beyond 65, more usually this is for financial reasons and all clergy have to retire at 70. At retirement some may wish to return to long-neglected interests or to take up new activities, not necessarily within the confines of church life. Others may discover new and unexpected dimensions to their calling, exploring fresh expressions of spirituality and faith. Those who still wish to continue active involvement in parish ministry may be appointed as honorary assistant clergy in the parish to which they retire, although it may be advisable to take a break of six months to a year before taking on such a formal responsibility. Others may be happy to take Sunday services and occasional offices on an ad hoc basis in the parish where they live or in nearby parishes. However, there is often a temptation for the newly retired person (and others who are anxious on their behalf or can see them as a useful resource) to fill the time created by retirement as quickly as possible. It may be more creative to keep that space open and to wait to see how God might want it to be filled.

Clergy, at whatever age they retire, need to be prepared to let go and make space for those still carrying stipendiary responsibilities. Stipendiary clergy should not retire to live in the parish or benefice in which they served immediately before retirement, but there may be some flexibility about returning to a parish from which they moved many years before. The guidance on contact with parishioners after leaving a parish applies (6.24). Some clergy chapters welcome retired clergy to their membership, but retired clergy should only attend chapter meetings if they are carrying responsibilities for ministry within their local parish or deanery and are invited to do so. Chapter meetings should not be seen as an escape from the loneliness and feelings of emptiness that may be an unavoidable experience in the early months or years of retirement.

Some ordained local ministers, non-stipendiary ministers, readers and churchwardens become more active in ministry when they retire from secular employment and have more time and energy available. For them this may be a late opportunity to give themselves fully to their vocation in a way that was not possible when they were younger. Theirs is a very different experience from that of someone who has spent twenty or thirty years in full-time stipendiary ministry. However, when the time comes for them to retire from office, those who minister on a voluntary basis may fear letting go of a long-established aspect of their identity and expression of their faith. Prayer, reflection and a willingness to consult with ministerial colleagues will all be part of discerning when it is time to let go of active voluntary ministry. Help and support may be needed as the minister adjusts to retirement while continuing to live within the same worshipping community.

6.27 Ministry towards the end of life

One of the consolations of ordained ministry is that it is a vocation which continues to the end of life, although the expression of that vocation may change radically. Ministers, like everybody else, encounter many losses as they grow older and face illness, infirmity and bereavement. Ministers who have spent their life caring for others and feeling in control sometimes find it extremely difficult to be dependent and may need grace to relax into receiving from others. Those who have spent their life sustaining the faith of others may experience a loss of faith and may need the grace to let others minister to them in their darkness. As with other aspects of bereavement and loss, ministers who have been a support to elderly people towards the end of life are not necessarily any better at living through the experience themselves. However, faith tested by doubt may be refined to its essentials, with a deepening of trust and a sense of growing closeness with God. The prayers of older and housebound parishioners play an essential part in sustaining the life of the Church and can be a vital expression of pastoral care. The same is true of the prayers of the infirm or housebound minister. The minister who has been faithful in prayer may become, in their increasing frailty and vulnerability, a living prayer. Their greatest work for God may come to fruition in old age, watching and praying, as did Simeon and Anna, for the fulfilment of God's promise (Luke 2.25–38).

Reflection – leaving the parish; retirement from ministry

- What is your typical way of taking leave from social occasions?
- How would you approach bringing your ministry in your parish to a close?
- What losses has your church community experienced in recent years and can you identify parishioners who have left without explanation or saying goodbye?
- If you have been in a parish where the incumbent left, how did the incumbent and the parish deal with the ending?
- How has your predecessor's way of ending their ministry affected your ministry?

- If you were to leave your current benefice, are there (a) parishioners whom you feel would be damaged if you were to cease all contact with them, (b) parishioners with whom you or your family would like a continuing friendship?
- How would you respond to requests to take weddings, baptisms or funerals after having left?
- If you are ordained, what aspects of ministry would you hope to continue after retirement?
- If you currently minister in a voluntary capacity, how will you decide when to retire from this role?
- Which aspects of ministry would you find hardest to relinquish as you become older? Which do you feel could grow stronger, despite age and frailty?

THE TASKS OF GRIEVING

Most theories about grieving focus on phases or stages of grief. These can imply grief follows a linear sequence when, in reality, its course is usually confusing and unpredictable. Worden's (1991) description of the tasks of grieving offers the grieving person some sense of how grief may be accomplished. These tasks involve:

- accepting the reality of the loss
- entering into the emotions of grief
- learning new skills
- reinvesting emotional energy

The tasks are interdependent. As the reality of death is absorbed, the grieving person begins to experience the intensely painful emotions involved in letting go. (Suppressing such feelings takes emotional energy needed for establishing new relationships in the future. Avoiding them by moving too hasitily into a new relationship or situation is risky, as they may have to be faced eventually.) A bereaved person usually has to learn new skills, such as cooking, financial management or learning to ask for help, and these can bring renewed confidence. Eventually, when the first three tasks have been worked through repeatedly, in many different ways, the grieving person will be able to redirect their emotional energy into new attachments or new interests. They may feel sadness and sorrow on particular occasions, but grief is no longer fearful or over-whelming, but part of life as it is now.

LEAVING A PARISH

The following guidelines for preparing to leave a parish are adapted from *Running through the Thistles* (Oswald 1978):

* plan a time schedule
* consult with others and identify tasks to be completed before leaving
* identify what will take most energy
* give particular attention to your own and other people's emotional needs
* identify support to help you and your family deal with your feelings
* identify the people you need to visit, phone or write to before you leave, particularly those who will find it hardest to lose you, those who have been especially important to you, and those with whom relation-ships have been difficult
* be aware that earlier experiences of loss and separation may resurface when a minister leaves
* be prepared for reactions of grief or anger, which seem 'over the top' in yourself and others
* be honest about reasons for leaving and realistic about your future relationships with members of the congregation
* do not avoid the pain of leaving by making unrealistic promises about maintaining contact
* be clear that, without exception, you will not be able to take weddings, baptisms or funerals after you have left
* be clear that you will not be visiting former parishioners in their homes in the parish in the foreseeable future
* record factual information which will be useful for your successor.

A Final Word of Encouragement

I pray that the sharing of your faith may become effective when you perceive all the good that we may do for Christ. I have indeed received much joy and encouragement from your love, because the hearts of the saints have been refreshed through you.

Philemon 6–7

Our caring for the people is our sharing in the present work of Jesus the Shepherd.

Michael Ramsey, The Christian Priest Today

Shepherding as described in the Bible is a demanding and sometimes hazardous occupation. It requires courage, as well as constancy and skill. The image of God as the good shepherd in Ezekiel 34 speaks powerfully of concern for the marginalized and a willingness to challenge and take risks for their sake. Pastoral care in our own day also requires courage and involves risk: the courage to be alongside others when they are in pain, feeling lost or confused and when their suffering touches our own; the risk of having no answers, only our willingness to be there (Campbell 1986).

Shepherds, living on the margins of society, were called to witness to the birth of Christ in darkness and poverty. But those shepherds were in company with one another, not alone. Ministers, often feeling marginalized by contemporary culture, are also called to witness to Christ in company with one another. There is no place for pastoral ministry in isolation. If our courage is to be sustained, we need to be constantly 'en-couraged' by each other.

Encouragement, 'striving with one mind side by side for the faith of the gospel' (Phil. 1.27) is a significant aspect of the ministry of the New Testament churches, and plays an important role in sustaining good practice in pastoral care.

In the Church today we are challenged to move from a model of ministry in which pastoral care is the responsibility of ordained ministers to one in which pastoral care is the vocation of the whole people of God. This brings many new opportunities to ministers, both ordained and lay. We need to learn how to be companions on this journey together, sharing our knowledge, our skills and our experience of the cost and rewards of pastoral ministry. But, in the words of St John Chrysostom (c. AD 386), 'Christ passed over all the marvellous works which were to be performed by the apostles and said, "By this shall all men know that ye are my disciples, if ye love one another."' Sometimes the very best pastoral care simply offers a loving presence, silently witnessing to God's love for each one of us. As lay and ordained ministers we need grace to trust that, despite our limitations, this may be enough.

Bibliography

Alcohol Concern, 2003, *Alcohol Problems Costing Britain £3.3 billion*, and http://www.alcoholconcern.org.uk/servlets/doc/282 (accessed 15 February 2006).

S. Atkinson, 2006, *Breaking the Chains of Abuse: A Practical Guide*, Oxford: Lion.

E. Berne, 1968, *Games People Play*, Harmondsworth: Penguin.

R. Bons-Storm, 1996, *The Incredible Woman: Listening to Women's Silences in Pastoral Care and Counselling*, Nashville: Abingdon Press.

F. Bridger, 2003, 'A Theological Reflection' in *Guidelines for the Professional Conduct of the Clergy*, London: Church House Publishing.

F. Bridger and D. Atkinson, 1994, *Counselling in Context*, London: HarperCollins.

G. Brown and T. Harris, 1978, *Social Origins of Depression*, London: Tavistock.

N. Burgess, 1998, *Into Deep Water: The Experiences of Curates in the Church of England*, Bury St Edmunds: Kevin Mayhew.

A. Campbell, 1985, *Paid to Care?* London: SPCK.

A. Campbell, 1986, *Rediscovering Pastoral Care*, London: Darton, Longman & Todd.

J. Chevous, 2004, *From Silence to Sanctuary: A Guide to Understanding, Preventing and Responding to Abuse*, London: SPCK.

A. Choy, 1990, 'The Winner's Triangle', *Transactional Analysis Journal* 20.1 (January).

Churches Together in Britain and Ireland, 2002, *Time for Action: Sexual Abuse, the Churches and a New Dawn for Survivors*, London: Church House Publishing.

W. A. Clebsch and C. R. Jaekle, 1994, *Pastoral Care in Historical Perspective*, New York: Aronson.

Convocations of Canterbury and York, Joint Committee Report, 2003, *Guidelines for the Professional Conduct of the Clergy*, London: Church House Publishing.

Department of Health, 1999, *Working Together to Safeguard Children*.

Department of Health, 2003, *What to Do if You're Worried a Child Is Being Abused*.

Diocesan Advisers in Pastoral Care and Counselling, 1995, *Standards of Practice in Pastoral Care*, Leicester: Vaughan College.

Doctrine Commission, 2003, *Being Human: Power, Money, Sex and Time*, London: Church House Publishing.

B. Fletcher, 1990, *Clergy under Stress: A Study of Homosexual and Heterosexual Clergy*, London: Mowbray.

J. Gosney, 2002, *Surviving Child Sexual Abuse*, Cambridge: Grove Books.

R. Green, 1987, *Only Connect: Worship and Liturgy from the Perspective of Pastoral Care*, London: Darton, Longman & Todd.

R. M. Gula, 1996, *Ethics in Pastoral Ministry*, New York: Paulist Press.

C. Hahn, 1991, *Sexual Paradox*, New York: Pilgrim Press.

C. Hahn and A. M. Nuechterlein, 1978, *The Male and Female Church Staff*, Bethesda: Alban Institute Publications.

M. Hill, 2001, *Ecclesiastical Law*, Oxford: Oxford University Press.

S. Horsman, 1989, *Living with Stress*, Cambridge: Lutterworth Press.

House of Bishops, 2001, 'The Mistreatment of Adults by those Authorised by Bishop's Licence to Leadership Positions in the Church', unpublished paper.

House of Bishops, 2004, *Protecting all God's Children: the child protection policy for the Church of England*, London: Church House Publishing.

M. Hunter and J. Struve, 1998, *The Ethical use of Touch in Psychotherapy*, London: Sage.

A. Irvine, 1997, *Between Two Worlds: Understanding and Managing Clergy Stress*, London: Mowbray.

P. Jamieson, 1997, *Living at the Edge: Sacrament and Solidarity in Leadership*, London: Mowbray.

John Chrysostom, c.AD 386, *On the Priesthood*, ii5, in *Saint John Chrysostom: Six Books on the Priesthood*, tr. Graham Neville, London: SPCK 1964, p. 63.

Stephen B. Karpman, 1968, 'Drama Analysis', *Transactional Analysis Bulletin*, 7.26, pp. 39–43.

Emmanuel Lartey, 2003, *In Living Color: An Intercultural Approach to Pastoral Care and Counseling*, London: Jessica Kingsley.

C. Lee and S. Horsman, 2002, *Affirmation and Accountability: Practical Suggestions for Preventing Clergy Stress, Sickness and Ill-Health Retirement*, Sheldon: The Society of Mary and Martha.

L. Leeder, 1999, *The Ecclesiastical Law Handbook*, London: Sweet Maxwell.

N. Leick and M. Davidsen-Nielsen, 1991, *Healing Pain: Attachment, Loss and Grief Therapy*, London: Routledge.

Legal Advisory Commission, 2007, *Legal Opinions Concerning the Church of England*, 8th edition, forthcoming, London: Church House Publishing.

R. May, 1972, *Power and Innocence*, New York: Norton.

C. Moody, 1992, *Eccentric Ministry: Pastoral Care and Leadership in the Parish*, London: Darton, Longman & Todd.

J. Nelson, 1992, *The Intimate Connection: Male Sexuality and Masculine Spirituality*, London: SPCK.

P. G. F. Nixon, 1976, 'The Human Function Curve', *The Practitioner*, 217 (cited by S. Horsman in *Living with Stress*).

Roy Oswald, 1978, *Running through the Thistles: Terminating a Ministerial Relationship with a Parish*, Bethesda: Alban Institute Publications.

E. H. Peterson, 1993, *The Contemplative Pastor*, Grand Rapids: Eerdmans.

M. Ramsey, 1972, *The Christian Priest Today*, London: SPCK

C. Rogers, 1979, *On Becoming a Person*, London: Constable.

P. Rutter, 1989, *Sex in the Forbidden Zone*, London: Unwin.

C. Saussy, 1995, *The Gift of Anger*, Louisville: Westminster John Knox Press.

G. Syme, 2003, *Dual Relationships in Counselling and Psychotherapy*, London: Sage.

J. W. Worden, 1991, *Grief Counselling and Grief Therapy*, London: Routledge.

F. Wright, 1982, *Pastoral Care for Lay People*, London: SCM Press.

Other resources:

Anglican Association of Advisers in Pastoral Care & Counselling, www.aaapcc.org.uk

British Association for Counselling and Psychotherapy, www.bacp.co.uk

Cruse Bereavement Care, www.crusebereavementcare.org.uk

St Luke's Hospital for the Clergy, www.stlukeshospital.org.uk

Society of Mary and Martha, Sheldon, www.sheldon.uk.com

Further Reading

General Interest

David Ison (ed.), 2005, *The Vicar's Guide: Life and Ministry in the Parish*, London: Church House Publishing.

John Witcombe (ed.), 2005, *The Curate's Guide: From Calling to First Parish*, London: Church House Publishing.

1 Aspects of Pastoral Care

D. Benner, 1998, *Care of Souls*, Cumbria: Paternoster Press.

D. Lyall, 1995, *Counselling in the Pastoral and Spiritual Context*, Buckingham: Open University Press.

D. Mearns and B. Thorne, 1988, *Person-Centred Counselling in Action*, London: Sage.

2 Power, Authority and Vulnerability

M. Barton, 2005, *Rejection, Resistance and Resurrection: Speaking Out on Racism in the Church*, London: Darton, Longman & Todd.

M. Chave-Jones, 1992, *Living with Anger*, London: SPCK Triangle.

E. H. Friedman, 1985, *Generation to Generation: Family Process in Church and Synagogue*, New York: Guilford Press.

C. Gilligan, 1982, *In a Different Voice: Psychological Theory and Women's Development*, London: Harvard University Press.

V. Herrick and I. Mann, 1998, *Jesus Wept: Reflections on Vulnerability in Leadership*, London: Darton, Longman & Todd.

A. Mindell, 1995, *Sitting in the Fire: Large Group Transformation Using Conflict and Diversity*, Portland: Lao Tse Press.

3 Boundaries in Pastoral Care

N. Autton, 1989, *Touch: An Exploration*, London: Darton, Longman & Todd.

H. Cloud and J. Townsend, 1992, *Boundaries*, Grand Rapids: Zondervan.

4 *Living Well in Ministry*

P. Ball, 2003, *Introducing Spiritual Direction*, London: SPCK.
P. Ballard and S. Holmes (eds), 2005, *The Bible in Pastoral Practice*, London: Darton, Longman & Todd.
J. Chick, 2004, *Alcohol and Drinking Problems*, Poole: Family Doctor Publications.
M. Guenther, 1994, *Holy Listening: The Art of Spiritual Direction*, London: Darton, Longman & Todd.
S. Pattison and J. Woodward (eds.), *The Blackwell Reader in Pastoral and Practical Theology*, Oxford: Blackwell.
R. Velleman, 2001, *Counselling for Alcohol Problems*, London: Sage
D. Willows and J. Swinton (eds), 2000, *Spiritual Dimensions of Pastoral Care*, London: Jessica Kingsley.

5 *The Minister's Personal Relationships*

P. Atkinson, 2004, *Friendship and the Body of Christ*, London: SPCK.
S. Walrond-Skinner, 1998, *Double Blessing: Clergy Marriage since the Ordination of Women Priests*, London: Mowbray

6 *Transition, Loss and Bereavement in Ministry*

S. Ledrum and G. Syme, 1992, *The Gift of Tears: A Practical Approach to Loss and Bereavement Counselling*, London: Routledge.
H. Ward and J. Wild, 1995, *Guard the Chaos: Finding Meaning in Change*, London: Darton, Longman & Todd.

Expanded Contents Listing

*Including chapter headings, section headings,
Reflections and supplementary material*